MW01268256

Fairy Tale to Murder

Fairy Tale to Murder

Satin Maize

Copyright © 2016 by Satin Maize.

Library of Congress Control Number:		2016902035
ISBN:	Hardcover	978-1-5144-5831-0
	Softcover	978-1-5144-5830-3
	eBook	978-1-5144-5829-7

All rights reserved. No part of this book may be reproduced or transmitted in any form or by any means, electronic or mechanical, including photocopying, recording, or by any information storage and retrieval system, without permission in writing from the copyright owner.

Any people depicted in stock imagery provided by Thinkstock are models, and such images are being used for illustrative purposes only.
Certain stock imagery © Thinkstock.

Print information available on the last page.

Rev. date: 03/16/2016

To order additional copies of this book, contact:
Xlibris
1-888-795-4274
www.Xlibris.com
Orders@Xlibris.com
734035

Contents

THIS BOOK

IS

DEDICATED

To those special friends, doctors, and adopted relatives who believed the truth and assisted my escape from my powerful, wealthy spouse who had murder on his mind.

PROLOGUE

THIS BOOK IS a fictional biography. Names, characters, places, and incidents are used fictitiously. Any resemblance to actual events, locales, or persons, living or dead, is coincidental.

CHAPTER 1

Early Childhood

M Y EARLIEST CHILDHOOD memories begin with me remembering crying in my crib after waking up from a nap. I distinctly recall looking around at the flowered wallpaper. Then I remember that I saw: my mother walked into the room, looked at me, and walked back out of the room. I would have been at that early navigation age, probably when you first learn how to roll over by complete accident. I had cried so hard and long that I was sweaty and my hair was wet. I never did remember when she finally rescued me from my crib. I do know that I was thirsty.

The next memory I have of my mother, who was my primary caretaker, was sitting on her lap as she sat at a table with two other women talking and having coffee. I was much older by now, about seven months or so. She was nursing me as she happily talked with her friends. She didn't seem to notice that I was having a difficult time breathing as her large breast was interfering with my petite nose. Mother took a picture of me when I was just learning how to walk. She snapped a picture when I was crying after she would spank my tiny hand for touching her doily. That is just how it was. She was somehow detached from being a mother, and I just didn't come first. She did.

She was somehow always on display. As a matter of fact, my mother would study store mannequins and try to model for my father in the same way these dolls were poised. She reminded me of a live mannequin who was stuck raising a child during the daytime hours while my loving dad was a salesman. She was very ostentatious about her appearance. Being tall, slim, and born with striking red hair put her at an advantage over other women. She got a lot of attention from men, but women hated her. Dad was trying to make a career for himself in sales to support his family. My mother had everything in order, and dinner was served at exactly six. I recall him showing me a lot of affection, and I knew he loved me at a very early age. Everything had to be prim and proper until after dinner. Then he would play with me by lying on the floor and tickling me. I really loved him. He would get down to the human level that she just could not find. I started to realize that when Daddy came home, he was very important to me and my mother. I went through a short stage when I would spill my small glass of milk each evening right after she would put me into the high chair. My mother would get so angry and upset that I messed up her perfect picture of life. My father would be silent too but then would give me a quick smile when she was not looking. I knew that I had better sit perfectly still as neither of us knew what she would do. My daddy told her to leave me alone, and he would try to assure me that everything would be all right since he was there. This nervous condition of mine did go away finally, but I do remember several episodes of it.

CHAPTER 2

Preschool

W HEN I WAS two years old, almost three, I remember my hair being shoulder length on pictures and watching cartoons in my little rocking chair while my mommy and daddy got ready to go to church. We went to Mass a lot. We attended each holy day and Sundays. Daddy told Mommy that it was a sin if we would miss one of those days. I was excused from this sin if I missed going to Mass because I was not considered accountable until the age of seven.

I remember the inside of this large church. I would stare at the stained glass windows that were above our heads on each side of the long church. I recall being interested in the sheep with horns, which really was a ram. I do remember the Stations of the Cross too. The priest would walk carrying a large cross to different areas of the church with two altar boys who were on his right and left sides. These young boys also lit the altar candles and would put them out with a long golden pole. There he would stop and pretend he was Jesus. He would then say a prayer at each station. We had to kneel. We got up and then knelt. We got up and then sat. The church was noisy with crying babies and the noise of the kneelers being lifted up and down.

The smell of incense filled the church as the priest would swing a big golden container filled with smoke, and he would walk from the front of the church to the back of it. He had two small altar boys on each side of him.

Communion was remembered with a lot of singing, especially Christmas carols. People would get up and out of their seats one person after another to form a line and follow one another to the front of the church where the priest gave the adults a white "Jesus" wafer on their tongues! I had to wait alone in our pew while Mommy and Daddy got up to get "Jesus" on their tongues. I was told that I had to be seven years old to make my First Communion.

We would drive home, and I would shiver until the car heated up. By the time it heated up, we were home, only eight blocks away. It would be dark, and Daddy would have to figure out where the keyhole was on the door. Then we were in, and the lights were on—including the real Christmas tree! We had a large gas furnace heater Daddy had bought that lit up and glowed after they turned it up! Mommy had wreaths with a red candle that lit up in each window. On weekdays, Mommy would stare out the window and worry whether Daddy would be late after the clock had turned six. Dinner was ready, and she was afraid that he would not return to us because of an accident. She never spoke of her fear. I felt it. He was always home by six. He greeted her with a kiss and then would say, "Where is Tinkie?" Then I got a big hug and kiss too.

It was at this age that when I was falling asleep in my bed with many comforters on and the windows were all frosted up, I saw a lion lying by my dresser. He lay there to watch over me. I told Mommy about this, and she listened to me. At this time, both Mommy and Daddy would kiss me good night and "tuck me in." I would make up a prayer to recite. The hall light was left on upstairs, and my door was left open several inches. Sleep would take over my entire body, and I would not awaken until morning. I do not remember mornings except getting dressed and making sure that my clothes were on right.

One good memory I recall was one very special snowy night when the snow was light and fluffy. My mommy and daddy put on their boots, coats, and mittens and gloves. With me dressed very warmly, with a wool scarf over my mouth and around my neck, they took me for a ride on my sled! It was warm, and the snow glittered under the streetlights!

Around Christmas, my uncles would visit. There were three of them. My mother's brothers. One of them died after getting a liver disease while in the military. He came too and brought his fiancée. Her name was Jennifer, and they were in love. He had given her a diamond heart to wear around her neck while he was away from her. They were to marry when he got out of the army. Instead, he died in a big military hospital. They never got to marry. My mother changed after that. She didn't care about church or pleasing my daddy. She loved her brother, and he had left her. She went to stay at the hospital, sleeping in his room for a whole week. I stayed with my grandparents because it was during Christmas. My father stayed home to work. They fought after that because Mother said that Daddy did not care enough.

On Saturday nights, my parents were happy if they had relatives to play cards with.

They ate peanuts and chocolate drop candies as they laughed and giggled! I was happy too because I fell asleep to their laughter!

Remember, I only knew my father's parents, not my mother's! We were Catholic like my daddy, and my mother's family was Lutheran. My mother's eldest brother and sister stayed with her parents and would not visit us. My three uncles, my mother's younger brothers, went both ways. Her youngest brother favored my dad and mom so became a part of us.

Summers meant less clothes and going to a lake to wade in the water with my blow-up toy that went around my waist! My parents and I went to a lake cabin for a whole week! Daddy worked from there, but Mother did not like the idea of not having a car! The old cabin had a wooden floor with cracked linoleum over it. The beds squeaked! We had a boat without a motor. Daddy rowed Mommy and me out to the lake with two wooden oars! I think we went out to eat because it made more sense than getting groceries and cooking in a strange kitchen! My mother let me stay in the sun way too long but blamed my horrible burned skin on it being fair. It ruined my vacation, but it happened over and over.

Our neighborhood had a lot of kids in it. We played softball in the street. We would fall and skin up our knees. Mom used peroxide to clean my wounds, and I wore Band-Aids. The only time we came into the house was to rest, eat, or drink! When the streetlight went on, it was time to eat, take a bath, and watch TV.

I played "house" with our neighbor boy named Johnny. I had a tent, and he was my "play" husband! Janna was my best friend. She would do things to irritate my mother. One time she took a fork and poked holes in our front screen door. Another time, she put her chewing gum on the steering wheel of my mother's new car! When my mother put her gloves to the wheel, they stuck tight to it. Janna got scolded often by my mother! Back then mothers wore hats to church in the summer, especially on Easter Sunday. They even wore corsages that were pinned to their dresses! Daddy would buy Mother an orchid to wear with a big hat pin through it!

We ate a lot of pop cycles! One day Janna and I decided to cut her hair. I took her long ponytail and cut it right off! Her father was furious! Her mother scolded me! We survived together. It was good to have a friend. I was alone before that and was directed by my mother to walk down the street to a house full of kids whom I did not know!

I carried a nicely wrapped gift and wore a pretty party dress but did not know who I was or why I was going. Lonely is not fun, and being the "only" child spells loneliness! My mother was not my friend. She was my mother.

Even though there were some happy times in my childhood, they did not stem from my mother. If she was happy, it was only at times when my parents were extremely happy together. My grandparents tolerated her, and my father was not going to give up his family for my mother. My mother was missing "herself." I don't think she developed an identity of being alone. Everything in her world centered around my father. She already disliked her eldest brother, her only sister, and her own mother. All of my life I heard how her mother "ruled the roost," and her own father was victim to it.

My mother had a lot of anger toward these people, and my father could not paint a perfect picture for her each and every day. It was not real life. At the age of four, I found myself playing a lot alone in an upstairs bedroom. I would pretend to be a mother with my dolls and cook in my childhood play kitchen. I would be there for hours. My mother would not disrupt me or request that we do something together or even have a snack! Her motto was "Leave her alone if she is content!"

I remember being between three and four years old, very young to remember but not old enough to understand what had happened to me on one particular day. As Mother was losing her memory, she had asked me if I remembered being four years old. She was sobbing relentlessly in her assisted-living apartment shortly after Dad had died of bladder cancer. She asked me to forgive her for the things she had done before she had become "saved" by Jesus. At that time, I really didn't recall the incident that she was referring to.

The recall went like this. I was at a preschool age, I think four. I had been playing alone for a long time. I recall my mother in a straight tweed skirt with a lime green sweater with nylons and high heels walking up the house stairs. I grabbed the hem of her skirt and tugged it once, saying, "Mommy, pay attention to me." She turned her head to her left side and looked at me. She then kicked me with her shoe, and I fell down eight wooden steps. I remember hitting my neck on the lip of the last step. I then fell forward, facedown into a pool of my own blood that would not stop bleeding from my petite nose. I did not know what to think or do. It hurt so bad. I screamed and continued to scream. She came down the stairs and stood next to me, not picking me up but rather shouting, "Quit crying or I will hit you until you do!"

She then cleaned me and the floor up, redressed me, and applied ice to my nose and added a Band-Aid over the bridge of my petite nose! I was completely tired and worn out by this time. She placed me at the dinner table. When my father came home, I was silent. He looked at me kind of funny, and I would not talk. Mother then explained to my father that I had fallen down the stairs, and she said, "Walt, I think Satin could have broken her nose!" She then added, "Doesn't her nose look a little crooked?" After this incident, much later as I developed as a child, Mother also remarked that one of my eyes appeared smaller, as it was not growing at the same rate as the other. This reminded her of this incident. I sat silent on my chair speechless. My chin met the edge of the dining room table. I remember saying to myself, *She is lying to my daddy!* I was so worn out and tired that I was just grateful to eat. Daddy would grab my chin and say, "Let me see your nose, Tinkie." I was silent.

When you are four years old or even younger, you remember incidents that were very severe. My mind did suppress these incidents during my childhood, but they were recalled around the age of twenty-five. I also know that I did not recall three very severe childhood incidents of parental abuse delivered by my own mother while I was growing up. A child does not retain a bad incident and learn from it. Their minds are not developed to learn from or prepare for another incident. They don't recall one bad incident to the next. Being an only child without siblings to learn from or advanced technology like today, only our instincts could guide us.

Since we are in my preschool phase of life, another very significant incident of abuse stands out in my mind. It was summer. My mother, my teenage uncle, and I were walking down our city sidewalk when my uncle asked Mother if I could have a Life Saver candy. She agreed to let me have one. As we kept walking, the candy slipped into my windpipe. I thought it to be odd even as a little girl. I pulled my mother's hand to stop walking. I could not talk but could breathe. It was lodged in my throat. My throat was very small to be lodged in. My uncle immediately grabbed me to swat my back, but Mother insisted that we keep walking to the drugstore as to "not make a scene" on the city sidewalk! We got to the soda fountain. My uncle then asked my mother if he could pick me upside down and hit my back. I stood waiting for the answer. I remember saying to myself, *She is going to kill me, and my daddy will not know what happened to me.* Well, thanks to my uncle Phillip, I am alive today. We had a bond. It was an unspoken one; he saved my life at four years old! Now I know the reason a Life Saver has a hole in the middle.

As for my mother, well, her karma was not very good. Her deeds were intentional. Her last twenty years of life were not good, nor was her death. We wished well for her, and I saved her life several times at the home where she resided, but I could not prevent her memory loss or how she passed away. Her Alzheimer's disease shut down her "gag reflux" in her throat, so her hometown doctor ordered the home to deprive her of food and water until she died! I think this had to be her karma. She was abusive to me and would not allow me to eat breakfast or snacks as a child. She packed my daily lunch and would not allow me to eat a healthy hot lunch at school either. To all of you, book readers, this is a display of bad karma.

After the broken-nose abuse and the slow reaction to the lodged Life Saver in my throat, I distanced myself from my mother. It was natural. She resented me more now, and my parents had taken me to get my five-year-old portraits done. There were four different positions of myself that the photographer took. I had a longer ponytail. My parents had them displayed in our house. My mother would look at each one and say, "Look at you, you think that you are so smart!" I did not understand her jealousy. She would tuck me into my bed at night with sincerity, but I remember waking up during the night and being so cold that I could not sleep. She would be angry and just tell me to go back to bed. It was confusing. When I was even younger, I would wake her up to go to the bathroom that was down the stairs, and I remember kind of falling from step to step. I was too sleepy to know if she pushed me.

I also remember my mother laying a large quilt on the floor. Then she would roll me up in it for a game. After I would roll over and over into the blanket several times, my head would be deep inside of it, then I was to call her to unroll me. The last time we played this game, she rolled me into the blanket. I cried, "Mom, let me out!" She stood next to me but stalled a minute before she let me out. I panicked and became afraid. Then she said, "See how lucky you are that I was here to rescue you!"

Again, more abuse when I was only four years old. My mother would want me to choose between loving her or my father. She would say, "Who do you love more, your father or I?" I did not know that this was a trick question with severe consequences should I not answer in her favor. I would say my daddy. Then her behavior toward me got worse. She would tell me that I was a bad girl, and honestly there was nothing to be bad about! Then she did the unthinkable. She would tell me that she was going to leave me forever and never return! Well, she would leave the house, get into her car, and drive away! I would panic and scream, crying for her at the front door, saying, "Come back! Don't leave me!" After I was totally in a panic, she would drive back to the house and tell me that she was giving me another chance to be good. I had done nothing wrong!

The despise and hatred, needless to say jealousy she had over my natural bond with my daddy, went on until I had my own children and my own spouse. However, she favored my brother since he was a boy, and she favored my firstborn son over my daughter! Simply stated because she hated her sister and mother. She went as far as to say that my daughter resembled her sister whom she hated. All of my life, my mother pretended to love but did not. She could only love my father who eventually found a mistress.

Besides the normal measles and mumps that children of that time got, I was physically sick a lot. I would feel a strange wave of dark energy hit me, and when I would look at any lightbulb in the house, they appeared to be a darker yellow color than they had been. If my parents would argue, this could happen, and sometimes it seemed that this wave of energy would just come into the room. My mother would blame my dad for my getting sick. She would say that he had been at my grandmother's house and had brought this illness home to me. However, it was not your normal virus. She meant that it was a spiritual illness that was transferred to our house from his contact with his natural mother. She wanted him to quit all contact with his mother. My grandmother was not at all evil but was "skeptical of my mother and her sneaky demeanor." She was a quiet woman who loved cooking, baking, gardening, and her children. She provided home care for her ailing and aged mother. Love poured out of her soul to me. I felt more comfortable being with her than at home.

I would run high fevers for three days or even up to a week. My mother seemed to like this. She would put two dining room chairs together with the seats facing each other. A blanket would be placed on top of the chairs. There I would be placed with a pillow and another quilt. This way I was on the main floor where my mother was. The focus was now on my mother being useful by being a nurse for her sick child. Every time I would feel this wave of dark energy come into our house, I would get very ill and would be too ill to walk. This business all stopped once I got into kindergarten. I do not recall it happening during grade school at all. My brother who is eleven years younger than I reported that it also happened to him during grade school. The principal had to call my parents as to why he was not attending school for as long as one full month. Again, Mother blamed this rarity of my father bringing this evil wave of energy into the family home. Again, she was made useful by taking care of her child.

When I started kindergarten, I was afraid. We didn't have preschool or anything of the sort.

My friend in the neighborhood named Janna did not have the same homeroom as I did. This was a big problem. My mother never tried to put us in the same class as all of the other mothers were doing.

My teacher had a boyfriend who was also a teacher in the next classroom. She would put on the record player and leave the room. I was aware of everything. I felt like I was supposed to be in charge of the whole class while she was courting her man in the hall. The record would be finished, and it would be grinding away until she returned. She seemed like my mother, very aloof. The other children were happy that they had new playmates. I knew that I was different from them. Well, I refused to go to school. I was scared and cried a lot. I would grab on to my parents and plead with them to let me stay home. This went on for several weeks.

One morning my mother had this brilliant idea that she was going to scare me even more by doing the unthinkable. She pulled out from under the dining room table one of the blonde-colored wooden chairs and made me sit on it in the middle of the dining room. I think she tied me to it with a handkerchief scarf that was either navy blue or red. They were popular back then for wearing around your neck or in your hair. My father stood wondering what she was trying to do. Then she kept going around me in a circular motion, screaming at me that she was going to put me in a mental institution if I did not go to kindergarten. She also made it a permanent solution by saying that I would board there and never come home again. This was even more of a tragedy for me to think that I would be separated from my father. I was too afraid to cry by now. My daddy finally said, "Tinkie, I will take you to the car." I have no recollection of what happened after that. I was so traumatized from thinking about school and then my mother wanting to "put me away" if I didn't go that neither option was good. I do know that my mother did talk to the teacher about her leaving the room and the problems that I was having. I did go to school after the teacher agreed to stay in the room.

My mother often did not pick me up from kindergarten on time. She was routinely late. Finally, the principal had to call our home to address the continual problem that was occurring. I remember standing in the long hall on the wooden floor while the janitor mopped it. My teacher stood with me holding my little hand. We both had our coats and mittens on. The school was empty except for the janitors. I saw how they emptied the classroom garbage.

We had our kindergarten concert on one particular afternoon. My teacher really didn't like me with all of these problems. She disliked my mother even more. We all had wooden instruments to play. All of a sudden, my teacher took me out of the group and sat me behind the blonde-colored piano. I was so embarrassed. I still wonder what I could have possibly done. I do not recall. My mother came to the concert with her good friend who was named Ann. Ann was from England and liked me but couldn't show it too much in front of my mother. I do not know what I could have done wrong, if anything, but was humiliated. When my mother got a hold of me, she scolded me for being a bad girl and embarrassing her. Ann said nothing. She couldn't; my mother was there. Ann was like a pleasant diversion for my mother, and she had to be sly about being my friend and support too. My relationship with her lasted until just before she died in Liverpool, England, on my dad's seventieth birthday, October 2. My dad died on July 5 at 12:01.

CHAPTER 3

Elementary School

AFTER KINDERGARTEN, I attended St. Ann's Catholic School in a small suburb of Milwaukee. It was there that I was loved and cared for by my very first teacher who was a Catholic nun. Her name was Sister Clare. She was like the shepherd to her little flock of first graders. Being kind, sweet, consistent, and diligent brought her respect and dignity. We just plain liked her. What a transition this was from my home life to a day of peace without anxiety. Now, I went home being filled up with love and learning. I had a purpose, and that was to be her student.

It was in the first grade when I met my girlfriend Shawna. She was very strong and secure. I wondered how this could have happened. I was not like that. In her family, there was a big brother at home, a mother whom she adored, and a father who loved her too. Her hair was a beautiful blonde color, and it was very long. She was a bit chubby, and I was thin with short hair. Her mother worked in a factory but was the one who made the money. My father was the parent who brought home his paycheck. Her mother and my father had something in common. They were the bread earners, so to speak. Her dad didn't seem to work very hard but was at home or in the garage. Her home became my second one. My mother liked this because I was not home. It was a perfect plan. Shawna would get food ready to prepare for dinner. She was a definite part of their family. I learned that she had another brother named Phillip. He was her big brother. He would tease her and protect her from anything. I was very envious of this situation. They had an old dog named Boot. I liked how I felt there, and Shawna liked having me as a friend. My dad gave her a lot of rides here and there with me. Her parents really liked that part of the friendship.

It was at Shawna's house that I would wear her mother's wedding ring for fun while she showered. Her mother was like us. Shawna had a best friend in her mother. I felt totally at home there and spent the next nine years there in friendship. Her parents also went on picnics with my parents and Ann and Woody too. My dad was the glue of relationships because he loved everybody. God sent me a new family, and I was happy. It was there that Shawna and I tried using a tampon when we were not old enough to use one. Her mom had to remove mine as it was stuck. We wanted to be big girls before our time. I think my father was glad for me too that I had a new friend and family. He had new friends too.

I now could eat at their house too. There were cookies each day and regular food. My mother was on a healthy food menu where there were no sweets or food between meals. I was thin until going to Shawna's house. We were best friends all through grade school, until ninth grade.

During our second grade, we ran into a problem. Shawna and I were split up and put into different classrooms because of a shortage of space. The school was going to move to a new one.

I lost my strong support that year. My mother had left the Catholic Church because the priest had fired her from working at the bookstore before Mass. She was humiliated and hurt. My father was not supportive of her either. He just didn't want to make waves with a priest. The priest was like God.

Life changed after that for all of us. Mom would not go to Mass. She and Dad fought over it for years to come. My first communion was not going well because of all the commotion. Dad and I went to church each Sunday alone. He then ushered to feel better about himself. I sat alone. He loved me though. My parents had violent fights, and Dad would threaten to kill her. When I went to school, I was afraid that he would kill her while I was at school. She would be dead and I would not have a dad. I could not concentrate anymore. Learning was hard. My teacher picked on me because my mother was now an outcast in the church. We were talked about too. Life changed for all of us from that year forward. I became anxious and nervous.

My third-grade year was good again. I had a lay teacher named Mrs. McCarthy. She was old, and her son was a priest. She ate a cheese sandwich on white bread each day at her desk. She treated me well and was very fair. My mother asked her if I was normal after all of the turmoil that I had gone through the previous school year. Mom came home from conferences with the good news that I was a healthy third grader. Mom was pleased.

My fourth-grade year was bad again. My grandmother on my dad's side had abruptly died of a heart attack. My dad was gone on a convention at that time. When he came home, my mother broke the terrible news to him. He cried for over three days, and there were teardrops on their bedroom floor that were left to dry on their own. I was sad for him, and he was not there for us during this time. Grandpa came over to our house and cried. My mother was not very sympathetic about this because she wanted Grandma out of our lives so she could have Dad to herself.

Shortly after Grandma died, my mother was happier. She became pregnant with my brother.

He was born when I was almost eleven. I was very embarrassed about this whole situation. I gained weight, and she would not let me shampoo my hair other than every third day. It was oily. I was going through puberty at this time. I developed what we called zits or pimples. I had acne very bad. My mother would take me to the drugstore and embarrass me in front of the clerk when trying to find a cheap solution for these zits. Squeezing zits became a new thing to do.

My brother was born and named Brett. My parents were happy. I was not. I was too old to inherit a brother. My uncle now lived with Grandpa so he would not be so sad. Relatives now came to our house to see the new baby. Great-Aunt Stella, who was my dad's favorite, came over to see if Brett would be baptized Catholic, since Mom was a problem with her religious rebellion. My mother now felt that she had an "edge" over the group because she had pleased my dad with a son.

I never really got to know my brother because they raised us as two separate families. She didn't want me to hold or touch my brother much. Her fear was that I would hurt him out of jealousy. Her protective custody of this new baby kept us apart for life.

At the age of ten or eleven, my mother insisted that she give me an enema. She would insert the long tube attached to a water bottle of warm water into my rectum and would make me lie on the bathroom floor with pain until I could not stand the pressure. I would call her to release me. I know that this was a part of her abuse. She also slapped me a lot across my face or on my legs in the summer when I wore shorts. After school, she would pick me up and take me to two separate women friends' homes. She did not want them to like me, only her. She called me the "devil child" and that I was of my dad, Walt. They would be kind to me but knew that they could not be too friendly to me. Their purpose was to listen to her woes of her terrible husband who was "brainwashed" with Catholicism. She would stay at their homes until late in the afternoon and pull into our yard a half hour before my dad would get home. Then the war would begin. He would ask her what she did all day. She had just gossiped about him, that was all. I never tattled on her or her abuse, ever. After being kicked down the stairs at four years old and being threatened with my life, I would never tell my dad what she did.

She also took me to my grandma's house, her mother's house in town. She was a widow. I did not know any of her relatives, except for Uncle Phillip and Aunt Fatima. She called her Mother, never Mom. My grandma made me banana cream pie. I remember being at her house very seldom when I was a preteen, once when I was about three years old. I did not know my own maternal grandparents, aunts, uncles, or cousins. One visit to the house on the farm was remembered when she told her brothers that I was of Walt, not her. They were not supposed to like me either. This coincides with her asking me when I was merely seven years of age to make a choice between her, who claimed to be like Jesus, or my daddy, who was like the devil. I had answered the question wrong. I had said that I chose my daddy since he loved me all the time. She despised me from that very second on. This did not stop ever.

The people in the church and town knew that she was weird. When she found Jesus and got saved, she was forcing pamphlets down people's throats. If they did not take one, she said that they were lost and going to hell. She was their only salvation besides Billy Graham. This news spread like wildfire. She was the "talk" before *The View* was presented on TV with Whoopi Goldberg and the other gals each day. I was singled out as her daughter. Plus, I lived in a house that was not normal, nor was it a fully built house. So when she got pregnant when I was ten years old, I was really embarrassed.

Every Sunday morning, there was a war between her and my dad. We went to Mass, but she stayed home to watch Billy Graham. She also sent Dad's money to these preachers. Her identity was out there, when she wore a very large crucifix around her neck. My mother reminded me of Lucille Ball and Dad reminded me of Desi Arnaz. Although they were not mentally ill, it was a popular television show, her with the red hair and him with the Cuban temper.

When I was about twelve, Mom took me into an expensive clothing store in our city. She was going to buy me a long coat for dress-up wear. I accidentally bumped into a clothes rack, and it tipped. I was so embarrassed. She moved away from me instantly and shouted across the store, "Satin, did you knock over that coat rack?" and then she laughed. I remember the Jewish owner and his wife being disgusted with her and feeling sorry for me. They did not laugh. It was holding only four coats. She scolded me when my girlfriends and I did not want her to walk with us down the street, as teenagers do. If we were older, I could understand it more.

Through all of this, I learned to let men take advantage of me in some way, but obnoxious women I have no time for because of her. Also, I notice every abused child and neglected child. When I walk through a mall and see a child or children tagging behind a parent, I want to grab the parent and ask them, "Just what the hell are you doing being a parent anyway?" I remember crying a lot.

When I was a preteen, she decided to provide me with freshly baked pie, saying that I had to eat it because she had worked so hard making it. Her philosophy was that I should gain weight so boys would not look at me. She called this being "fleshy." So I went from being starved as a child to overeating as a preteen. She of course, fasted, not eating for three days to keep her weight in control so she could model new clothes for my father. This was known as her spiritual fast for the Lord.

I was instructed not to study. The Lord would miraculously give me the answers on a test. That did not work. I was getting Cs, not As, on my tests. I learned to leave the house, sit in the car, and smoke cigarettes. I smoked in the bathroom, and I know that she could smell it. Never did she say a thing about this. At sixteen, I went out with a strange boy who had zits all over his face. This was okay because his dad owned a business. When the most popular boy and his friend came out to my house to play football in seventh grade, she was rude to them and told my dad that they had bothered her by getting cake crumbs on her kitchen floor. They could not come back. I could not go to the movie or dances with popular boys in my class because I was too young. Then I was not to go out with Catholic boys in the first place. Of course I had gone to a private Catholic school for grades 1 through 8.

Staying away and underage drinking in bars in other towns were acceptable because I was not in her house. She went as far as to say that I was not going to college because she did not go. Besides, women only went to college to waste money and meet their husbands. That explains her telling me to quit pretending to be a nurse when I was about five years old. I would fold a tissue in half, pin it to my hair, and pretend to be a nurse. Her comment was "You think that you are going to be a nurse, huh? Well, you are not. Take that Kleenex tissue off your head. If I couldn't go to college, you are not either." Now it all makes sense to me. I was told not to study and to gain weight in seventh grade.

My father had a few words to say also. Don't ever bring a black boy, lawyer, or non-Catholic home. My mother said I could not date a Catholic. If I got pregnant or joined the military, I would be disowned. When you are from a small family, those are big words. I should have run and kept running.

I resented them and their protectiveness of my little brother. When he was born, she said that I belonged to my dad and he belonged to her. The wedge still stands between us even now, although we know of all of this sickness.

CHAPTER 4

Junior High School

I WAS POPULAR IN seventh grade, especially with the boys. I had lost weight, had long dark brown hair, and was confident within myself. When my mother would come to the Catholic school to pick me up but would suddenly drive away, I was not bothered anymore. She could not hurt me with this kind of abandonment anymore. I was not attached to her in that way. She would see me coming out of class and then suddenly drive away. She would come back within ten minutes, saying that she had forgotten eggs. I didn't care anymore.

At sixteen, she slapped my face, and I told her that I was going to call a social worker to report her. That was the last time she would hit me. However, she did order my father to enter my room and hit me repeatedly because I complained that I could not sleep with my dad's snoring. Our walls were paper thin with no insulation between them. There was wood paneling on all of the walls. We lived in a '60s basement house that was buried with earth on the west side but open in the front on the east side. It faced the lake that ran into the river. It had a kitchen and eating area, living room, furnace and utility room, cellar room, bathroom, and two bedrooms with one storage room. One had to walk down a hill where the cars were parked without a garage to the front door. They did not have money to build the upstairs or the garage. So I was singled out in school as the kid with the weird family. My classmates would come out for my birthday parties and ask if I lived in a snowbank. I always had good parties and food by this time. My parents seemed to like the activity. Dad was always happy to see the kids and give them a ride to their homes. He never complained about this ever. He liked being alone in his car.

In our school, a Catholic-run school that went through eighth grade, there was no defined junior high school. It was odd. I thought our self-identity was not defined as having grown up into young adults. So my classmates had known me since first grade. We all had our opinions about each other.

CHAPTER 5

High School to Marriage

F ROM BEING COMFORTABLE in grade 8 to changing to a public school for grade 9 put me in a tailspin. I had trouble adapting. The kids I had known had now spread their wings and had developed friendships with the kids from public school. I lived two miles out in the country and had to depend on my parents for rides to school. I had no other choice but to take the bus home. I did not develop as I should have. Remember my mother prevented me from hanging out with several girls and boys in grade 8 because she was jealous. She had demanded I stay in my room on a Friday night when I always got to go out before because a certain boy along with other kids had invited me to join them for a movie. I remember it to this day. The torture I felt and the happiness she gained! She was a witch. Her actions were never about me or my good. It was all about her and how she gained pleasure by being in control.

There was no intention for good for me from my mother. Neither parent had a plan for me to go on to college. They only wanted to keep me from dating as long as possible to avoid teenage pregnancy. My father started lining up men for me to meet at the age of sixteen. He was an ugly boy who had very bad acne who was my first date. My dad had lined him up with me because his father was the owner of a very large company.

At eighteen, I had two girlfriends. We went to a nearby town to underage drink in a bar. On Sundays, we went to the same town for teenage dances. I met a guy named Richie. His family owned a business there, so my parents encouraged it. I loved his family and had a friendship with them. I loved them more than I did him. After high school, I needed to get away to find myself. My mother did not want me to come home on weekends, so I went to Richie's house. Just as she always wanted me to stay at Shawna's house during my school days, now she did not want me to come home from Airline School. She wanted her little family of my brother and dad to herself. No wonder I did not develop a relationship with my little brother! After her telling me not to waste their money by going to college, I dropped out of Airline School to marry Richie. There was no reason to live miles away from where he worked with his dad. After the courtship and the dating, marriage was a huge loss for me. I was not educated beyond high school, and neither was he. My mother did not want to see me much after the marriage. That was nothing new. If anything, I gave her a new place to visit. With no education, I became very depressed. I told my father of my mistake, but he firmly announced I should live with it.

I stayed six years. It was during that time I obtained my AA degree at a community college by working summers. Richie also wanted to go to college but did not want to work a full-time job plus go to school. He then stayed in his pity and only wished he could have had a college degree. He was only twenty-three at that time. Every day was the same. I did not feel comfortable with him because he had no goals or dreams. I felt like the hands of the clock continuing to go around and he was just there.

I was drained and wanted out. I left and stayed with my parents for six weeks with their blessing. It was then I moved again to finish my education at the age of twenty-six. I then found myself poor and living with kids who were right out of high school. I was a nontraditional student.

CHAPTER 6

University Life

H ERE I WAS twenty-six years old with students who were nineteen. I felt out of place with them but knew that I was on the right track. In one week, I had gotten a job as a waitress in an upscale supper club. It was there that I met Juan. He was a bartender. He was interested in me from the get-go, and there was an instant attraction. We spent the wee hours of the morning in my car in front of a local cafe chatting away. It was not long and we had sex. It was awkward. He was using me, I think. Who knows? I thought that I was pregnant; he thought that I was on the pill. I was not protected. I felt pregnant and did not get my period. Juan took his fist, made a face, and punched me in the abdomen. If I was pregnant, I was no more. I had skipped my period for two months at that time. I was told that I had had a spontaneous abortion. He aborted it with his fist. I could not study or think; and I was angry at myself, him, and life. A baby at this time would have been poor timing. He was studying for his bachelor's degree, as was I. We were older and on the bottom. Juan came from a professional family. His father was an inventor and engineer. His brother was an engineer. The oldest brother was an MD, and Juan was the "black sheep" of the family but very loved. His mother was unique and accepting. We traveled to the state of Washington for Christmas. I loved Juan still, and we had grown very close as lovers and friends. I was extremely naive about life, and he was not.

He was handsome, and I was in love. The unwanted pregnancy was put in the past for now.

There came the time when Juan proposed to me in the same cafe where we had had our first date.

I told him that I could not marry him because he was crazy. He was diagnosed manic depressive after an accident. That is what I meant. I did not think he was serious, but he was. Our relationship deteriorated after that. He left for the summer and broke my heart. The heartache lasted a long time. We were connected for about six years. He called me each year. It only reminded me that he was not with me.

CHAPTER 7

My First Career Position

I SUCCESSFULLY LANDED A wonderful job after having graduated from college at the age of twenty-six. By now, my confidence was a bit higher. Juan was left behind in my memory bank. I had met another young man named Ben in the grocery store. He helped support me financially and had a family for me to get to know. He had an older half brother who was disowned, but I liked him and his wife. They had two children. His father was very handsome and elderly. His mother was very heavyset and had had a stroke. She was evil. They had Jeffrey, Paul, Ben, and Tim. Ellen, his mother, said each boy had to get married in sequence. The oldest had to marry first and then right down the line. She herself was a fruit loop, if I ever saw one. Ellen was very jealous of me and did not like the attention that I got from her husband. Ben and I lived together, and she hated that. She hated it so much that we decided to elope and get married. Where I came up with that idea had to come right from Satan himself. We flew to Las Vegas on a weekend and got married. Ellen almost had a nervous breakdown. She said that we had to get our marriage blessed in their church. It was a Missouri Synod church. I think we did. That really didn't do the trick for her though. She called Ben many times a day. He would scream at her. We had a small reception in our apartment building where she slapped my face prior to it in the ladies' room. I don't recall what had been said, but she showed her authority with her hand. Each day she would call me and tell me that I would be divorced by April 1. Why she picked that day, I will never know. She was a witch, with energy that would make Satan cringe. We got married, never slept together, became violent with each other, and went to a counselor who told me that I had to divorce Ben because of something he had told him in a counseling session.

Ben had a guy friend whom he worked with. One morning I found the two of them sitting on the living room floor in our apartment touching each other's butts, laughing and watching porno movies. I was stupid enough to marry this guy and buy a house. Steven worked with Ben, and he would come over in the morning and walk right into our bedroom while we dressed. Nothing was sacred. We did not have sex anymore; they did. Ben was gay. I didn't even know what it was. Apparently, Ben's mother either knew this or provoked him into this lifestyle. This occurred before the "gay movement" became popular. I lived with Ben until May, out of pure spite for his mother, Ellen. Ben moved into the new apartment building that Steven lived in. Of course they lived across the hall from each other. I refused to give up Ben. Then I did the unthinkable: Ben and I bought a house together. I never saw Steven again until he was on the city police force. I decorated the house, and my new husband did some remodeling. It was nice. Never did I as much as walk around the perimeter of the house before I divorced him in the spring.

I would go to my sales job feeling alone and isolated. It was awful to say the least. He worked nights and slept during the day. I worked days and slept during the night. We had a cat named Scarlet. I was simply beside myself. We avoided each other like the plague. I would find *Playboy* magazines piled high under the bed. Ben's mother was so happy sharing the good news that her curse had come true and we would finally be divorced as she had predicted.

I found myself driving in my company car with the rain pouring down so heavily that the windshield wipers could not keep up. I was sobbing and scolding God why I could not live in a rich neighborhood with a responsible husband whom I could have children with!

CHAPTER 8

The Meeting

B Y NOW, I was looking for a way out of this whole mess. How could I have been so ignorant?

I was not blessed with intelligent parents who guided their child but rather blamed me for anything I got myself into.

Now, I had met Marc through a girlfriend who was getting a divorce. She had two young elementary school–aged girls. We became friends through church. I visited her lovely home often and listened to her woes in reference to her husband. She was attractive and intelligent and divorcing a man who had plenty of money. I was aware of her lifestyle and elegant home. On one particular day, she invited me to her home with several other people. She had a plan to meet a new man. She didn't want to have him at her home alone with the girls just in case her husband found out about it. She feared that he spied on her and could get custody of the girls. So I agreed to come out that evening for dinner. I met a few other women and one particular man there. She was engaged in a very heavy conversation with this man about his divorce and her upcoming one. I was naive to all of it. I knew nothing about child custody issues or divorces where there was a large amount of money to split or spouses who cheated the other partner out of what should have been rightfully theirs. The two of them sat and hashed over their divorces and pending dissolutions.

The man, who was large in size, kept talking about how crazy his ex-wife was and how she could not take care of their children. They were so engaged in divorce talk; neither one of them realized that there were other people invited to the gathering. We, the guests, were definitely used in this plot for this woman to meet this particular man. It was a setup.

I told this man that I too was worried how I would manage alone when getting a divorce.

A concern of mine would be that I feared not having a good male friend to lean on for support. He listened but was very nervous or on edge. I also told him that I was concerned how I would get my physical needs met. That is when his ears perked up. He liked sex and was having an issue finding women for that too.

This particular large man offered to take me home after I told him that I was leaving my spouse. He dropped me off at my house where I still resided with my gay husband. He didn't seem to be attracted to my appearance but rather that I had sexual needs too. I was pretty, though. For once in my life, my weight was perfect. My hair was long, dark brown, and healthy. I dressed well. To him, I was a person to have sex with. He knew that I was legally married and respected the word "marriage." He said that he would take me on a date every Wednesday night before and while I filed for a divorce. He knew I did not have money. My friend had filled him on that. She really had an edge over me on that one. I had nothing and was getting nothing, plain and simple. She would get a home, money, and custody of her children, she hoped. Her fear was that she would not get her rightful share of their marital assets. By using this planned gathering at her beautiful home on the lake, she had hoped to entice this large man into a relationship with her.

CHAPTER 9

The Date

MARC, THE BIG man, was very quiet during our movie date each Wednesday night. I don't remember much about them. I know he held my hand. He did not like the fact that I was still married. The first time I approached his house, I realized it was the same house and neighborhood that I had found in the rain only days before. He would secure a babysitter for his son, Jake. That was the first time that I was out with an adult male who had to seek a babysitter. He lived in an upscale neighborhood where the neighbors complained if they saw a tissue on your lawn. It was winter. I had not been in houses of this nature except with my parents when they viewed the parade of homes when I was a young child. The outside was all brick, and it had fancy front lights on a brick gate in front of the circular driveway.

After about a month of Wednesday night movies, he asked me to come to his home about five o'clock. I did. There I found his son, Jake. He was sitting at a large kitchen table, which was actually made out of wooden floor. Jake was somewhat chunky in size and had a part between his two front teeth just like I used to. That was before I took the initiative to cut the cord between my front teeth, in order for them to grow together because my parents would not pay for braces. Having a big smile on his face, Jake said, "Are you going to marry my dad?" I said, "I don't know." He kind of caught me by surprise. The popular game was called Dungeons & Dragons. There was a neighborhood friend over as well.

I had brought with me on this date a homemade flower arrangement that I had just put together before arriving. It was in a blue polka-dotted coffee cup. Marc was flattered with my skill and thoughtfulness. Off we went to a movie. After the movie, he brought me back to his house to make love. I loved it and knew that with his touch and that special feeling inside, this would be my husband. We had two sexual episodes of the same nature that meant to both of us that this felt right. Now, I was basing my beliefs on the fact that this man was mature, intelligent, established, financially stable, and ready for me to be a wife. I believe he had told me that he was ready to "fill the slot" for the new wife position. This all happened so fast. I went back and forth to my sales job on the road and would check into my residence too.

On one particular night, we had heard a noise in Marc's garage. There was somebody shuffling around. He called the police. By that time, the intruder had left. About a week after this incident, I went home to find my husband asleep. He had worked the night shift, and nothing seemed unusual. Ben had basically used me financially to buy our house. After the purchase, he had absolutely nothing to do with me in any way. I was married less than six months.

It was in the early afternoon, and I quietly stepped into the bedroom to find clothes in my closet. I gingerly slipped downstairs to take a shower. As I walked out of the shower, dripping wet, slippery, thin, and cold, I was jumped by Ben and grabbed by the throat and thrown down on the floor. With his two hands around my throat, he tried to strangle and rape me at the same time. I fought for my life by digging my fingernails into his back. I was afraid that I would lose my job had I reported it. Immediately I knew that the intruder at Marc's house must have been Ben. I immediately called Marc and told him what had happened. He told me to pack my belongings and come directly over to his home. It was there we nestled in together. From that moment on, we were in a relationship that lasted for twenty-five years–almost.

CHAPTER 10

Our Live-In Situation

AS STRANGE AS it sounds, Marc and I got along wonderfully. It was amazing. He made love to me after a month of going to a movie every Wednesday night. I was still legally married to a bisexual man who used me financially to buy a house. I was alone and isolated and found friendship in a woman who by accident introduced me to my future husband of twenty-five years. There I was in this man's house. This raised a few eyebrows in the neighborhood, and news spread fast that Marc had a new love. The mother-in-law was the first to receive the news from Jake.

We were happy, in love, and in sex; and our relationship felt just like we were meant to be together forever. His son, Jake, was intrigued with this whole situation and told the world about his dad and new girlfriend. Marc and I made love in front of a blazing fireplace, which was in his master bedroom. We were chemically intertwined. I knew from the start that this was a mature man when he had to take a babysitter home. He was a mature, professional businessman who had traveled the world. I, on the other hand, was an attractive tall woman with long shaggy brown hair, which was in style at that time. Also, I possessed a good job that entitled me to a company car, expenses being paid, prestige, and power within a national company by calling on key accounts in my city. I had to have a college degree to obtain this position. The company had good profit sharing as well. I stayed with this company for five years until six months after our firstborn son had arrived. I was the only woman in a district of twenty-eight men. They were all my dad's age but very warm to me, except for my boss who was named Jo. This man was a person who actually said that women should stay home and be barefoot and pregnant. I later tried to get him for discrimination as he picked on me and always spied on me or my whereabouts but did not do so with the other men. This work relationship lasted for five years. He would scream at me from across the parking lot as he hated me so. Marc was happy that I brought in a paycheck and was a sales representative.

The neighborhood ladies, who stayed home as they were married to medical doctors, used to visit with Marc since he was raising his son alone. They all stopped coming over after I had arrived. Marc blamed me for this, but it was most common to do when a girlfriend had moved in. Several of these women were neglected wives with husbands who were so responsible that either they wanted to tune them out after they came home or these wives were just plain ignored. They found solace in their friendships and common problem with their important husbands. I was younger with no children and not married, so I really did not fit in with their clique. One doctor was so fussy that he asked me to pick up a tissue that had fallen on our lawn from my purse.

Our relationship took off so fast that after I got my divorce, I found an apartment but ended up renting it to my brother for his college years. I spent time baking cookies, cooking, doing bookwork, and purchasing our first dog together. I was the girlfriend who lived with Dad. Eleanor finally visited and met me with Andes, Marc's dad, and she "minded her p's and q's" by keeping her mouth shut. However, she spent time discussing this new situation with her friends, her other daughter-in-law, and the mother of Jake. I was the outcast with her. The first display of her was the fact she came over and cooked. I liked it. This was not an intrusion for me in any way.

Our dog was an Alaskan Husky with beautiful blue eyes. We named him Cinder. This dog lived to be seventeen years old. Marc had to put him down at that time, and his remains were in an urn behind his desk at the office.

Jake's mother, who was named Sue, was beside herself because she wanted Marc back. They had been divorced for three years before I arrived on the scene. I thought this was safe, but as time tells all secrets, I found out different. There was another businessman who also wanted a relationship with me, but he was married with two kids, the youngest only two years old. I did not want to get involved with a married man. Now I think back and know it probably would have been a better bet than what had happened in our marriage. I almost lost my life. Later, I reacquainted with this man for emotional support for six months as Marc left me and was having an affair but I did not know with whom. Marc told me that he looked at relationships like a pie. Each person got a piece of him. He was the pie. I thought that this was a strange concept to live by, and it did affect me, which was for sure.

Our dating courtship went on for a year, and then Marc proposed to me saying that he loved me and wanted to get married. It was like a deal with love, but the catch was that I would have to sign a prenuptial agreement. I waited until two weeks before the wedding date to do this. It was not that he owned a lot but rather that he did have equity, and sizable too. His parents were wealthy. The wives did not work out of the home. I could not get used to this at first. The family had a sizable business that employed many people in the city. They had actually, at one time, owned three separate outlets in two other states. The wives did not go to the plant. This was the old school. The wives made the dinner, went shopping, entertained, cooked or hired a cook for the family functions, and kept their husbands comfortable. We all drove fancy cars, but the husbands drove fancier.

Marc did not buy me fancy gifts at all before the wedding except for the two-carat engagement ring. He even made me pay for fixing his parents' ceiling of their California home after I swung a golf club in the living room and brought down a section of the drywall. I remember him buying me one dress, period. The diamond was luscious and a showpiece to all. That is what he liked. Everything had to be big in size or worth to show the rest of the world who he was and what he could afford.

My parents liked him because they thought that I would be well taken care of. I was financially. I did not have to look for family either. He had one. There was a sister and brother with a sister-in-law and their kids. He also had an extended family that he shared with me, and I liked it. We attended all kinds of family functions and holidays. He had an adorable daughter named Liana who visited every other weekend, and I loved her so. I loved her from the first time I met her. We had an instant bond. Her little tennis shoes had safety pins with beads strung on them. She lived with her mother, Sue. Soon she wanted to live with us. She would always be sad when she had to go home to her mother. Not because she didn't love her mom but the action was at our house. Her mother bought her a puppy to make her happy. It was very difficult for her to go home after a weekend with Marc, Jake, and me. She wanted to be in this new family, and I wanted her to be there too. I was really getting close to Liana, and Eleanor did not like it because she wanted to protect Sue, the natural mother.

CHAPTER II

The Wedding

WE DECIDED TO get married on December 12. This was to take place in Marc's home, which was not financially mine. The neighbors, who were doctors' wives, helped me out with a dress designer in our city. The designer made two dresses for me. One was for the wedding night on Friday, and the other was to be worn at the Sunday party. The actual wedding dress was a pink-striped knee-high gown, which had a lace jacket to wear over it. It had spaghetti straps and revealed my thin arms. A rose was designed and worn as a broach on the lace jacket. I wore a brimmed hat with veil over the front, which was made from the same lace as the jacket. The white fitted long gown had many covered buttons, which ran down the middle of the back, and transparent material covered the whole back and part of the front. It fit snugly to my shapely body.

Our cleaning lady, Maggie, came prior to the ceremony with her sisters to prepare our Sunday brunch that was held at our new home. The Sunday evening meal took place at a local dinner club. Everything was lovely, and we all had a lot of fun. We held our ceremony in our living room with a county court judge performing it. Several of the family members were not happy about it as they still carried a torch for the ex-wife, Sue. Marc was very nervous. I was calm. However, I felt that there was a secret that several knew but I did not. I shrugged it off and went on with the ceremony. Liana primped in the mirror with me, and we took a picture of it. Jake, on the other hand, refused to get dressed for it. Marc's dad wrestled with him to button his buttons.

The wedding took place as scheduled with light snow falling. Our neighbor plowed our driveway for us. We worried that snow would keep guests away. The great-aunts, cousins, brothers, sisters, sisters-in-law, parents, grandpa, and close friends poured in. It all went very well. Our life was like a fairy tale come true.

I had signed the prenuptial agreement only two weeks before the wedding after Marc had said that only if I signed it would he let me raise our two children in my religion. I had no choice, as I would not forfeit my Christian religion. There would have been two families disowning their adult children if we had not done it this way.

CHAPTER 12

The Stepfamily

LOOKING BACK, MARC and I had decided to start blending me into his nuclear family. This was really a big bite to chew off. Jake was being influenced by his mother and paternal grandmother not to like me. Liana and I were forming a close bond. I hated to see her leave on the weekend, especially after Marc and I married. Jake would come back from his visitation hating me, and it would take a whole week to get him back behavior-wise on an even keel. So to include me in this little family, Marc decided to take the three of us on a winter vacation to California. The kids were eight and ten.

This was quite a trip. Marc made a new rule during the car ride. Both kids had to sit on their side of the backseat. One arm had to be on the door rest with a distance between them. Liana would copy Jake, and he would slug her. Whoever followed these instructions would get $10 when we got to our destination. They knew what money was and followed the plan. We took the kids to Disney World and had a remarkably good time. This was my first encounter with stepparenting.

I had learned in a blended family group later that stepparents do not have any rights. I changed the rule as I was raising Jake. I was tired of him saying, "You are just my babysitter." It was not his fault as his mother was working on him. At one point, we kept her from visitation with her own son because of her bad influence. Since the kids lived in two different households, there was a lot of jealousy between them. Liana was younger than Jake by eighteen months, and of course he was her elder. When she would copy him, he would become very angry. At one point, he grabbed her hair and pounded her face headfirst into the butcher block in our kitchen.

Another time, he took her head and put her neck between the door of the refrigerator and kept slamming it on her neck. I thought this was quite violent, even for jealousy. He was angry because his family was split up. He had always hoped that his parents would get back together. This is common for children to wish for. Jake resented me until he was sixteen. Then it all changed for the good.

The family was unbalanced. It was very lopsided. Marc had a family who supported him all the time, no matter what. We had everything, his family, our family, and Jake. Liana lived alone with her mother. At one point, her mother dropped her off in the summer with a suitcase that contained fall school clothes. What she was trying to say was that she likes it there and you might as well just keep her.

Jake looked forward to going to his mother's house for his visits. His mother and he were close. Liana looked forward to coming to our house too. The jealousy continued between the two siblings. Grandma Eleanor doted on Jake. She made this very apparent. One time she let Jake hit Liana over the head with a toy guitar right in front of me. Then I got involved, and she came up with this question for me: "Do you want to be in my family, Satin?" She was letting me know that it was either her way or the highway. I replied that I was supporting what was right.

Eleanor also tried to convert me to her religion. She was the Jewish matriarch of the entire family. Over all of our married years, I found out just what kind of power she had. Marc had me sign a prenuptial agreement that was in his favor, protecting him from monies that he had not yet earned. To negotiate or steal from a person, one always finds the other person's weakness. My Catholic or Christian religion was very important to me and my family. So Marc had said that I could raise our unborn children Christian if I signed his prenuptial. I stalled up until two weeks before the wedding. Marc was so crafty that he actually drafted the prenuptial one night on a legal pad. He then had me take it to a lawyer of mine who would actually draft it up. This made it look like I had actually sold my own soul away instead of him doing the "dirty" work. It was taken to a lawyer who was very young and just beginning his career. He told me not to sign it and that he definitely would not sign it if it had been him. I responded back, "But I love him, and he won't marry me unless I do." It was signed. You see, I trusted Marc. Actually, I needed my own lawyer who would counsel me throughout my twenty-five years of marriage so I would never make another mistake trusting my husband or anyone else.

My parents thought that I had nothing to lose, only to gain. My father never trusted Jews. He went as far as to say that he did not believe that the Holocaust had ever existed. He, of course, didn't tell Marc this. It was contained between my mother, my brother Brett, and me.

CHAPTER 13

Blending the Family

I WAS BLESSED WITH a wonderful girlfriend who had three children and four stepchildren. Her name was Jean. This woman was a godsend to me. She taught me how to be a mother. We talked about everything, and she was a stepmother too. Her spouse was a doctor who had lost his wife. He had never gotten over it. She did not like feeling second to the deceased wife and mother. However, the four of us had a really good time as we laughed and told jokes over dinners out. We remained friends for five years until she got a divorce. We had gone to a cabin with the kids, and Jake got poison oak on his face. It was painful and swollen for a week. He had to fly to California to meet his mother in an almost-unrecognizable face. Jake's mother, Sue, resented this whole new situation and shared her information with one of our neighbors. This neighbor had a son who was Jake's best friend. All of our news went to that house and the children for at least ten years.

Jake loved to tease me. Having a new stepmother was a new positional link in the family system. Now we differentiated between family members because we were a nuclear family and a stepfamily. There was hurt and rejection everywhere. As much as Marc and I were happy, the ex-wife, Sue, did everything to cause trouble. Soon Jake was acting out and telling me that I was just a babysitter. He soiled his underwear and spit watermelon seeds in my face. One day he got into my company car with his friends and drove my car through the neighborhood. I was running alongside the car trying to convince him to stop the car. He just laughed. He was ten years old, and so were his little buddies. Marc did not discipline him often because he felt sorry for him. We fought for years over this child and his lack of being disciplined.

Grandma Eleanor spoiled Jake so. He was her first grandson and could do absolutely no wrong. Also, Sue, the ex-wife, was considered to still be in the family as their son divorced her. I had all of the cards stacked against me. My own mother sided with my enemies; and Marc, who should have supported me, stayed aloof. I was alone without support. Thank goodness I had a good sex life with my husband. Our sexual chemistry helped us out.

Marc and I had a lot of fun entertaining. Pictures were taken regularly. My parents were over a lot, and we all went to see them, an hour away. Mom made a great meal for all of us, and we played card games with the kids. Liana loved my parents and stayed with them for a week in the summer. They loved her and doted on her. Jake liked my dad but not my mother. He was taught by his maternal mother and grandmother where his loyalties really belonged. As time went on, we had developed a very fine family.

CHAPTER 14

I Am Pregnant

I WAS PREGNANT WITHIN months, and our son was born on January 8. We had wrapped gifts for a boy or girl baby and did not want to find out the gender ahead of time. Liana went to my gynecologist with me on visits to see the fetus move on the screen. She was eight years old. On the day we found out about the pregnancy, Marc had sent flowers to my hotel room as I was still working as a sales representative for a major food company. They came in a delicate basket, which was carefully arranged with pink and white mums and red roses. Marc was happy to be a father again with his new pretty wife. After my fifth week of pregnancy, I got so sick that I was bedridden for six weeks. The day I received the flowers, I went to brush my teeth and felt a male hormone so strong in my body that I became weak and had to lie down for an hour to complete brushing my teeth. I was in for five months of pure hell.

When I first found out that I was with child, we were elated. However, after the sixth week, I became very ill. Waking up with a nauseous stomach was a daily routine. This episode lasted for five months. My gynecologist gave me something to drink before getting out of bed. I lived on Chinese noodles. My mother gave us a baby gift. I would not look at it. Marc was enjoying a cup of chicken noodle soup when I grabbed it and threw it at him. I was so angry that this special time was making me so sick that death would have been better. Each day, I woke up with the plague of morning sickness. It lasted all day and every day for five complete months. I had to go back to work to keep my job. It took me a long time to shower and dress. Coffee was out, and I had to switch to tea. Hot roast beef sandwiches became the meal of the day and month. I had gained weight from 135 pounds to 206 by the time I gave birth to our son, Josh. After the birth, I lost forty pounds in one month.

I will never forget the time that I had checked into a hotel room for the evening after work. I was as big as a house, very pregnant, wearing a moo-moo gown, standing with my back to the door while I adjusted the heat register. To my surprise, a businessman walked into my hotel room. I went completely hysterical on this man. He was so afraid that he came forward to console me. The closer he came to me, the louder I screamed. He briskly grabbed his suitcase and raced out of the door. I could have delivered that baby right there. Shortly after this incident, I went on maternity leave.

My water broke at dinner one evening while I was bending over to wipe up dog urine from the bedroom carpet. Jake was there and was home with me. Marc arrived shortly and took me to the hospital. I was claustrophobic since childhood and found myself stuck in an elevator with Marc and the Candy Stripe girl who escorted us to the birthing floor. We sat for fifteen minutes; I was in a wheelchair and realized that I could not move. Marc and the aide looked at each other and pushed the red button. Finally, we went up to the sixth floor.

Labor was the most awful thing I had experienced up to now. It went on for at least six hours. I was swearing at the world and agonizing in pain, asking how could women possibly have more than one child in their lifetime? I had one neighbor lady brag how she walked into the delivery room. Every woman had a story to tell. At the end of my pregnancy, I could not keep my legs together when I sat. Eleanor had bought me my maternity clothes, to my surprise. She had told Marc that she had enough grandchildren and didn't need any more.

Josh was born with natural childbirth as the nurse had given me my epidural injection too late and it did not take effect until after Josh was born. Also, Josh was delivered with his right elbow pushing through my birth canal. After this was finally over, I asked my doctor for an aspirin. The nurses treated me like royalty. I was called Mrs. Silverstein. I was soaking in the hospital sitz bath when I heard one nurse talking to another nurse, saying that Mrs. Silverstein had delivered a fine, healthy boy. I felt very different and important. Marc was noted as a VIP on the patient registry. His family owned a large business in the city, and I was his wife. Our name was well known.

I looked at the little baby lying on my stomach all bloody and wet while my husband and the doctor were coaxing me to nurse him. I had a quick lesson on colostrum, the thick orange-yellow fluid that appears in the mother's breast after giving birth before the milk comes out. The nurse taught me how to feed this little guy so he would not suffocate. It was a big deal when my milk came out as I was afraid he would starve on this colostrum. Everything was a new experience for me but not for Marc. He had gone through this two times before with Jake and Liana.

Parents came; the new infant was the first on my side of the family. Eleanor flew in from California to see her sixth grandchild. Pictures were taken with my face looking like a blowfish, swollen and puffy from pushing a little elbow through the birth canal. We all felt very different. Marc posed with his mother, who was holding the baby. We had gifts, flowers, money, and cards from all over the United States. Marc ran an international business. Our nursery was paid for by a business associate. There were baby showers. Savings bonds were set up for the baby.

The homecoming was quiet and peaceful. I had requested to walk down six flights of stairs, but the nurse said I had to take the elevator. The cart was full of flowers and balloons. We had the baby in a new nursery at the top of the stairs, but I cried because it was too far away. Marc decided to make him a bed in my original baby buggy. That worked for us as he was at the end of our large bedroom. Jake asked me if Josh would be his brother forever before he invested in a new relationship with him. Jake was a very intelligent kid. I reassured him that half-blood siblings are forever. He held the baby carefully and was very attentive and interested in him. They were bonded from the start. Jake was eleven years older than his new brother. Little Liana came to visit two weekends per month. Marc went to parent-teacher conferences, and this was very new to me. We attended elementary school concerts and programs. Marc carried his new son around like a football in public.

I now was on maternity leave from my sales position. My boss came to greet the baby, and a savings account was established for my new son by my company. Each representative put in money for our new little guy. We had become popular ever since the balloons hung on our mailbox in bundles of blue for a boy. I spent my day dieting, nursing, reading, cooking, and being a babysitter to Jake. Marc traveled after we had this baby and left Jake and me alone with this baby for one week. I got the flu, and he failed to call me for a whole week. I thought that was very strange. Now I look back, and I know it was strange. My six weeks went fast. It was very difficult to go to work, especially traveling two-thirds of the state.

CHAPTER 15

Our Move to Twenty-Fifth Avenue

J AKE WAS GETTING older by now and was a teenager. He resented the fact that he lived with us and we had sold his home. We really did not understand at that time. Also, his mother was leaving our city to live by her elderly parents in Florida. Jake wanted to leave with his mother. I begged Marc to let him go, but a stepparent has no rights. I lost the vote. Jake rebelled, and life was torture. Jake loved little Josh. That is what saved him. The love between the two boys grew and grew. Liana went to live with her mother in Florida, and I felt like half of my heart was gone. This was awful. We were rid of Sue and her energy, but now we had Jake rebelling because of her departure.

By now, we had sold our house and were living in a house rental. I was never a part of selling the house or any of the details. I was just told that it was sold. I never knew the asking price or the selling price. Everything went on behind my back. This was a problem in our relationship. It was like everyone but the wife, me, knew what was going on. With this method of treatment, I did not learn either. I learned about families and their behavior. I guess this was a continuation of my social work background. When Sue would call and argue with me about Jake, I would get so exhausted that I would have to take a nap. This woman was a psychic vampire. Laugh now but find out later that I was right. She would drain you of every inch of energy that you had in your body.

If you met her in person, she would glare into your eyes and drain you of any energy that you would give her through eye contact. She was a big problem during this time. I was glad she was leaving our state to reside in Florida with her aging parents. With her, she would take the little girl that I had grown very attached to. Liana didn't eat much but did like tuna. She said her mother fed her breakfast cereal. We didn't know what to think. Was she getting her protein or not? Who knew?

Sue did not go unnoticed in our area. When she came to pick up Jake, she was still driving the car that Marc had given her to leave their marriage with. The color was a bright yellow. She stuck out like a sore thumb everywhere she went. I never wanted to be like her. There was no boyfriend in her life either. It seemed as though men avoided her like the plague. She was very verbal about sharing her bad child custody case with teachers, ministers, and the general public. At one point, Marc had asked me to go to one of Jake's parent-child conferences until he arrived. So I did. The elderly lady with a stern lip and gray hair told me to leave because I was "just" the stepparent and that the "real" mother had just left her classroom. The friends of Jake and their parents had to be either on our side or on Sue's. There was war going on all around us. My whole marriage to Marc was an ongoing conflict. I could never put out the fire. It was not until later that I really understood who the arsonist was. I was living with him. Marc always made a big deal of it when he would write out a child support payment to her. Sue shopped at Dillard's for Liana. Really, he had caused all of her grief.

One day Sue actually came into our house when she had dropped off Jake from his weekend visitation. She went upstairs to his bedroom. Another time she came over and walked in with Jake's jeans that were not dried because her dryer broke. At that time, Marc called her into the kitchen in front of me and told her that this was not her house and that it was mine. Sue was not living in reality at this time; she started to tremble and almost fainted. Then she left the house. Later came the guilt trip that now she knew that Marc would not be coming back to her; he was married and even had a child with his new wife, which was me.

The story Marc had told me and my parents about his former marriage was that his wife suffered from serious depression and that she had been hospitalized for months before he was forced to divorce her for fear that he would too be drained and unable to sustain himself or his responsibilities. Stupidly enough, we all believed him. He was so convincing. Besides, Sue was a bit different. She was eccentric, noticeably different in style and speech. I noticed that her support seemed to be her mother who resided out of state and a girlfriend who lived only blocks from our recently sold house.

He had filed divorce papers on her while she resided in the psychiatric unit of the local hospital. Her diagnosis at that time, he said, was clinical depression. We always believed what he said. We are taught at an early age to trust the ones we love, right? From my background, I should have known better.

I had seen pictures of Sue and Marc dating. He loved her because she was thin and attractive. She finished college; and he quit, married, and raised children, which lasted for him to be a very long time.

CHAPTER 16

Marc Wanted to Build

ALL OF A sudden, Marc wanted to build a new home. I really didn't know why. I had asked him to finish the basement. He did not want to put money into it. So he said that we would build a new home. So he scouted about to find land. He was always resourceful and intelligent. He came up with ten acres of beautiful woods in the city limits of Milwaukee. With a good purchase price in hand, we bought the property. Then the excitement started. We went to open houses in upscale Milwaukee to get building ideas. I was never an equal partner in any money decisions. I did not know what he had or what he was acquiring in his business. Marc would have me come into the office and say, "Sign this." I would respond, "What is this?" He would say, "Just sign this or I'll divorce you." Matter of fact, I do not remember when his pretense began to show up in our marriage. I just knew that I was stuck. My prenuptial read that I would have to leave the household should a divorce occur. Usually children remain in their own house. He held this over me all of my married life.

So when we were building this house, it did not belong to me. My parents thought this was okay since there was so much wealth involved, like there would be plenty to go around should something bad happen. However, I got a forewarning from Marc's aunt. She said to me at my prewedding shower, "God help you, girl, if you ever get a divorce," as she walked away, shaking her head.

I spent a lot of time picking out wallpaper, tile, carpet, paint colors, draperies, cupboards, sinks, faucets, stain colors, and kitchen and bathroom hardware and designing a fancy fabric headboard for our oversized master bed, plus anything else that came up. By this time, we had moved to a rental house and had sold Marc's present house. He had his present house to accommodate himself and his son, Jake, after his divorce from Sue. This had infuriated Sue. She had lost a marriage, her position, half of her motherhood, losing Jake to Marc, and now was degraded to a house that was half the price of hers. To top it off, she had to contend with a younger woman who was raising her son. Not to mention, her own daughter had bonded to this threatening woman.

First Sue tried to be my best friend, thinking that she would see her son more than what the court had set up for visitation. She was not honest with her feelings either. Her true feelings would come out on the phone by screaming at me or crying to Marc. He savored this. After doing damage control, he would try to console her in front of me. It was an act in his play. My parents felt sorry for her. So I did not get support from them over any behavior problems that I was having with Jake. My parents liked Marc because he was taking care of me and they had a grandson. Their life was now complete. My brother was not yet married but dating a woman he did marry.

We had the neighbors over for a Halloween party, but I never really felt like I fit in. I was at least six years younger than the parents. They were nice enough, but we had nothing in common. If the women had worked in their past, they wanted to sweep that under the carpet now as they doted on their successful husbands and their careers. These successful medical careers provided them with lovely homes, unemployment status, position, power, country club activities, and children who could go to any college they wished. They had a head start into the lifestyle that I was just learning about.

I was invited to the holiday luncheon with the ladies but did not feel comfortable. I really had nothing in common with them. There was too much of an age difference between us as well as employment status. I had my sales career at this point, and they were all housewives. Well, I am proud to say, I never became like them; I remained true to myself and my friends and always talked to or greeted acquaintances from the past and present. To this day, none of these women will address me in public. Oh, how glad I am that I never became affected, as Marc called it. Marc and I shared the same feelings on this one. Both of us talked to people from all walks of life.

CHAPTER 17

Happenings While Living on Twenty-Fifth Street

MARC WAS A self-made man. He obtained his business knowledge from his father and Uncle Ben, among other entrepreneurs. He read a lot, listened, and applied what he would learn. Add a few people skills and you have a great salesman. However, he was cutthroat, which was quite fitting to the business he was in. I was preoccupied with raising little Josh and contending with Jake's anger issues. By now, I had a girlfriend to share motherhood and stepfamily issues with.

Summer had passed in our rental unit, and fall had approached. Our new home construction had gone smoothly, and we were scheduled to move into it by Christmas. Our furniture was in storage, and we were living with the bare necessities. Marc hated it and was not used to anything but posh living. I, on the other hand, had moved many times during college and had camped, backpacked, and vacationed in the wilderness. I adjusted to any situation I found myself in. My father used to say, "Sis, you can make any place look good." I loved to decorate. Matter of fact, when our "big house" was nearing completion, Marc would shower there.

At this time, I was trying to get pregnant. Marc had no interest at all. I did not want our children to be over three years apart. He had stated that he only wanted one child to bond the marriage. I did not want Josh to be alone as I had been raised. I was right on this decision. This time I had difficulty getting pregnant. I sought medical help and took the drug that could result in multiple births. After using this medication for a couple of weeks, I did conceive another child. At one point, I was supposed to take a sperm sample to a chemist when it was still warm. I let it get cold because we got company. So I heated it up in the microwave. I took it to the lab in the rain on a Saturday, standing there with a jar of scorched sperm. The lab technician replied, "What did you do to this sperm?" I confessed that I had heated it up in the microwave. He acted like I had killed a person. He should have thought, *How is this woman going to be a mother?*

It was out of the blue that we received the unthinkable news that our new home was on fire. Marc answered his cell phone, only to hear the original owner of the development telling him that they had called the fire department because they could see flames rising above the trees. To rise above the trees would mean that the house had been engulfed with flames. We scurried to the site and witnessed the blaze, and I watched my husband break down and sob. A neighbor guy who owned a famous tavern in our city stood and laughed. I looked at him and said, "God, you deal with this man."

He did later. That particular man lost his business and his wife. The kind neighbors near the site took us in and handed us a tissue box. At that point, Marc was still in shock; I was quiet, and I tried to comfort him by saying, "We were not in it. We have our lives." Nothing made him feel better, not even food. It took three fire departments to put out the blaze, and it burned for over one week. The house contained seventeen rooms and a four-stall garage. The fire had started during a lightning storm early Saturday morning on Labor Day weekend. Later the fire marshal had reported that lightning had struck the chimney area and had ignited the wood shingles. The fire spread rapidly in the great room as it was seventeen feet tall. Marc made a call to the builder to confirm the amount of insurance he had carried on this property. It was confirmed to be one million. Yellow police tape was strung around the burning house that sat on its own ten acres of wooded terrain. The loss was covered by insurance.

The tragedy was devastating to Marc. I was just glad that we had not moved into it yet. We were safe. Our personal belongings were intact. That is what mattered the most to me. However, the builder took a long vacation to Hawaii, I think. It was over a month that he was out of sight. In the meantime, people from the city came out to view the ruins of the beautiful home destroyed by fire. The carpenters, plumbers, electricians, cabinet makers, drywall workers, neighbors, firemen, and city officials all came out to view this tragedy. Parents came out with their children to show them what fire could do. Beautiful autumn was not so beautiful in our woods. Autumn came and went; the house stood untouched for months. Marc spent his time at his office. He came home for dinner and watched TV and visited with me and the kids. He played with Josh. When I look back, we were not really close in our relationship. He was close to our bookkeeper, however; her name was Sandy. I was pregnant, but we were not close. I did not suspect anything, but I should have.

Soon it was Halloween, and we took pictures of the kids going out for trick or treat. I still had my parents only an hour away. Marc's parents resided in California at this time. My girlfriend and I were like sisters, and I was not at a loss for sisterhood. Marc was at work talking on the phone to his customers and Sandy. I had told him to hire her as she was a proficient office girl. However, they worked alone every day. She was overweight and plain, but she had an essence about her that people liked and felt comfortable with. I would stop into the office from time to time and she would be pleasant.

I had our dining room table refinished while we lived in the house rental on Twenty-Fifth Street. I had it delivered back to our residence within a couple of weeks. It looked great. All of the scratches and indentations were gone, and it looked like new. It had been given to Marc by a friend. The top was made from an actual wood floor. It was worth refinishing. At this time, Jake was very angry about his mother moving out of state. Marc would not let him join her. We even asked Sue if she would consider trading the kids for a while. She refused completely and would not even hear of it. So Jake was angry. He had lost his home, mother, and sister by physical proximity and instead was living in a rented house on the other side of the city. We were dealing with his rebellion and rightfully so.

One afternoon, I had left to go pick up little Josh from day care only to find the newly refinished chairs had been all marked up. There were deep gouges in a circular motion on each seat of the chairs. I was beside myself. It had to be Jake doing this because of his retaliation in regard to his mother leaving him behind. So I did the unthinkable: I went to the Salvation Army and picked out a cushioned chair that Jake would be allowed to sit on since the destruction of the chairs had taken place. Sue, his mother, went behind my back saying that I was humiliating him and hurting his ego. So what was I to do? Marc left everything up to me. One day I was washing laundry. As I poured bleach out of the bottle, my toothbrush came pouring out. Jake had put my toothbrush in the bleach bottle. Now I did not have a toothbrush. Jake busted a lamp shade, and he was mad. By now, he was fourteen and good in size. He hated me and was rebelling about all of these changes that were impacting him and us. Marc was dealing with work and rebuilding the house. I was a mother dealing with Josh, Jake, and pregnancy. Later, Jake told me that he was bleaching his jeans with the toothbrush, and it fell into the bottle. Within a couple of weeks, Jake used my toothbrush again, and it was filled with breakfast cereal. He did these little irritating things that you would have to wonder if they were intentionally done or just plain stupid acts of adolescence. He hated buttoning his buttons and wore picture tee shirts like all of the other kids.

Marc wanted to visit his parents. At this time, Jake was in school, so Marc said that he was old enough to stay alone while we were in California. The truth is that Marc would have never stayed alone without me at home and did not like his office without Sandy present. He had asked Sandy, his office worker, to give Jake a ride to and from work plus check on him. I also had our cleaning lady check on him. He was feeding our dog potato chips, not dog food. Both he and the dog survived, and Marc didn't care if the house had burned down or not; after all, it was just a rental.

CHAPTER 18

Moving into the Big House

I BARELY REMEMBER THE day we moved into the "big house." This is a blur to me. What I do remember was that little Josh was only three. The house was so large that I provided night lights on all of the stairs and hallways. My local arts group used our house as a fund-raiser on a home tour. It raised over five thousand dollars for a scholarship. Little Sharnell was born after we had moved in. She had a lovely nursery upstairs on the east wing. I made myself a bedroom across from hers so I could collapse there after her nightly feedings. She was a good baby. I was never sick from the pregnancy, and taking care of her went smoothly. By this time, Liana didn't like living in Florida with her mother. She wanted to live with us. Marc and I decided to try to seek custody of her through the court.

Mother-in-law Eleanor thought this would be devastating to Sue. Then again, Sue would not negotiate any other child custody arrangement. We went ahead with our plan. I was interviewed by the county social worker to prove my skills in raising Liana. I was approved for being her ongoing parent in our home. By now we had a lot of enemies. They were Eleanor, along with Sue and her friends, parents, and grandparents. I was really absorbing the stress. This was not what I needed after giving birth to little Sharnell.

Sue had hired a strategic female lawyer to defend her rights as Liana's custodial parent. Liana had to run away from our house and go to a children's home for one week before we could go to court to retrieve her. It was awful. Sue and her lawyer were saying that Marc had kidnapped her. So Liana could not be in our house or Marc would go to jail. Marc then instructed his daughter, who was thirteen at that time, to get on a city bus, pack one week's worth of clothes, and go to a home for runaways that he had found for her until he could figure out a legal procedure to take. It was difficult for any child to come to a parent's home for comfort and stability only to find these people telling her that she would have to get on a bus, go to a strange place for runaways, and wait for further instructions from her dad on when he would get her released.

Here she was being bounced around like a rubber ball with her own parents fighting over her residence. I hope she has suppressed this ordeal in her consciousness. She has to be living with many emotional scars. It worked out, we thought; she started her junior high year from our home. How did this happen? Marc called on a judge who actually signed an order for him on Labor Day weekend. This was a personal favor for the so-called "family." Did I belong to the mob by connection?

Liana was feeling very bad the day that I went to the halfway house to bring her more clothes. She was in a strange place for a strange reason. Here was a perfect student, with good morals and values, with no criminal background whatsoever, staying in a strange place and city with adolescents who were in trouble with the law or who suffered abuse. She was withdrawn when I pulled up to the place. She was walking with the group in a line, head down and looking like a forlorn girl. I had to be strong and reassure her that Dad was working on things on her behalf and she had to trust him and be patient. I really felt sorry for her. But later I felt sorry for us because by gaining her custody, we had really stirred up a can of worms. Now we were in for a big surprise. It was not about her but her mother, her maternal grandmother, and my mother-in-law, Eleanor.

There was no support coming our direction for taking this huge stand. Marc's relatives thought that Liana should remain with her mother. They feared that her mother would suffer a nervous breakdown. Marc had some reservations too but wanted to please me, his wife. I had my hands full with Jake, Josh, and Marc; and now we were taking on a custody issue. I was given a weekly allowance. It was not a lot for what it all included: groceries, gifts, clothing for all of the kids, or anything that came up. I think the amount was about $350 per week. I saved money by doing my own pedicures, manicures, and hair; cutting Marc's hair; and doing some cleaning.

Our house was huge. It was 6,200 square feet. We had seventeen rooms, including six bedrooms, a very large kitchen and eating area, a formal dining room, a solarium, a formal living room, four bathrooms, a master den, a laundry room, three stairways, a catwalk, a children's family room, a screened-in porch, a large foyer, a four-stall garage that was carpeted and finished, two furnace rooms, and a front porch. We also had a large metal shed that held two cars and storage. The home was nestled in secluded woods beyond a newly established neighborhood. I can still feel a thunderstorm brewing all around the big house. It stood tall and safe after it was rebuilt again after the initial fire had flattened most of the home. It was surrounded by trees completely yet cleared about sixty feet from the woods, allowing sunshine and blue sky to enter. Rebuilding this home took a four-month period. The first phase of building took six months. This time, Marc had lightning rods installed on top of the cedar shingles. He also installed a metal fire wall between the two sections of the home. Lightning did hit the house about seven times after the initial attack that destroyed the beautiful home. There was no significant damage done during the later attacks of natural weather occurrences.

Our home was absolutely beautiful. We designed it and decorated it as we wished. At that time, Marc made a lot of money in his business. His parents always wondered how he had so much wealth. I did too. After all, at the time Baby Sharnell was born, we had built a new home on Lake Michigan and had this very expensive home in the city limits of Milwaukee. We did not socialize with people of the same financial category either. He wanted to be regular in the scheme of things. So I had friends of my choosing, and so did he. We then created our own family of friends separately.

I grew up in a low middle-class family. He grew up in a mildly rich family. His father and uncle had done very well in their business venture. Business was their background no matter how you looked at it. My father-in-law, Andes, would sit on the toilet and add up numbers in his head for fun.

Marc took after both of his parents. He was kind and business-oriented, loving basic math like his father but nurturing yet cunning like his mother. Her brown eyes would become beady and small when she despised you. I knew them well.

My parents, Lucille and Walt, visited biweekly to share a meal with us and play with their grandchildren. We all enjoyed this. Marc was good to them, and it was reciprocated. Since his family was in another state, he welcomed my family and was happy that the kids had grandparents. Life was good. We were all together, and Jake and Liana were bonding as siblings. Liana worked very hard on this. The big kids loved the little kids, and the little kids loved the big kids. However, we were still having trouble with Jake. He hated me and was rebelling for many reasons. I was equally angry at him for staging fights between his dad and me. His mother was really working against us in every way she could. I slapped his face, and he slapped mine. It was awful. I was tired of his messy room and not picking up. I suggested a military school, and Marc said no and instead sent him to a Catholic prep school out of the city. He drove back and forth and stayed in the dorm. Then he went on a foreign exchange program to Germany. Jake was very intelligent. He too possessed the natural math skills from his ancestors. He did not have to study but still made the honor roll. Liana, on the other hand, had to study to achieve her honor roll status. She would come home from school, eat, and go to bed until 5:00 a.m. By setting her alarm, she would arise to do her homework.

I remember taking Baby Sharnell to a popular photographer in downtown Milwaukee for her one-year-old picture. She wore a white dress with a large collar made of pink and white polka dots. It was garnished with white lace. She had a little mark on her right toe from a blood sample taken. She wore a silver bracelet on her right hand. Sharnell was a very quiet child. I went to her nursery when she was six months old and looked into her little brown eyes. I then asked her to talk to me. It was only after that I witnessed her cooing as a baby does. She lived in a household of six people with everyone doting on her most of the time. I was so large as a pregnant woman carrying her. I recall holding my stomach as I walked down the stairways. Josh, then three, would hide behind my large moo-moo gown. I did not nurse her because Jake was sixteen, and I thought it would be inappropriate to do so. Also, this way the kids could share in feeding her for bonding reasons. However, nursing does create closeness with a mother and child. I instead rocked Sharnell in her white wicker rocker and sang a song that I had made up each afternoon with her bottle feeding. It still did not create the closeness that nursing my son seemed to do.

Liana came home from school. It was her first day of junior high school. She asked me to give her my hand to bond. She said her bonding with her natural mother would be broken by living with us and that she did not want to be alone. I reached out my hand to her. She was actually transferring her energy that was connected to her mother to me. Sue was so distraught after she lost custody of her daughter that she met a group of Wickens who told her that she could get her daughter back by using the power their coven would provide her if she joined their cult. She was living in Florida with her elderly parents. She had taken Liana there to reside with her and her parents. Liana wanted desperately to come back to Milwaukee. This arrangement was all right for a vacation but not for a living situation. Liana desperately wanted to come back to us and her familiar surroundings.

After school started, the big kids settled in quite well. Jake stopped causing trouble, and Liana settled into her studies. Baby Sharnell, well, was a baby. Josh was three years old now and really liked the attention from his big brother and sister. He was now in competition with his little sister for Mom's lap. Marc was busy at work making money to support this family of six, including him. I cooked, cleaned, shopped, and was a mother, wife, and daughter. We had birthday parties, couple of friends over, and did some entertaining. Marc and I always went out for dinner each Saturday night. That was our night for intimacy. It was routine and timely on Saturday night. Our sex drive was less as we dealt with the stresses of work and raising children. Eleanor tried to be supportive to us over our new child arrangement, but really, she was fretting it. Sue was depressed in Florida and living with her elderly parents. I believe she was trying to get a job. Most everyone was envious of us. We had a million-dollar home that had been rebuilt after the fire, and now Marc had bought some lakeshore property and had a new house built on it for our summer vacations. Who would not be jealous of this situation?

Both of our families were wondering where and how Marc made so much money. We had some fine neighbors on the lake. An older couple who took interest in us and our growing family had become our friends. I often had coffee ready for the elderly man who was named Vern. He loved to see our cute kids. The older kids liked their freedom at home while we were away. At times, I would stay at the lake for four days with the kids alone. It was always the kids and me everywhere. Marc was a businessman and did not have a computer at the lake. This was his excuse for not spending a lot of time there. The kids and I loved it. We would walk through woods and flowing creek waters near the house. It was common for black bears to rub against the house as they made their way to the water in the wee hours of the morning. I had to wind the windows in so they would not disturb the sleeping kids in their bunk beds.

CHAPTER 19

The Evil Begins

W HEN IT WAS Sharnell's first birthday, I took her to a well-known photographer in the city for her photos. As I was coming out of the sitting, I felt a strange stillness around me, as though I was being watched. I could feel a small group of people concentrating on me in a not-so-good way. This feeling never left. I was psychically being watched or followed. I had not felt this type of thing before. Also, I could not feel Marc either. I had always trusted him and Sandy at the office. From that minute on, I felt invaded upon and as though someone was in my own protected energy field. I became tormented by this and felt alone.

By now I had sought out psychic healers to explain to me just what I was experiencing. We would go through a buffet line with our family at the restaurant on the lake and a piece of melon would taste like poison. I had to spit it out. Weird things began happening in our home. Marc also felt strange. He would get a splitting headache and would become so weak that he had to lie down for several hours. We were being attacked by something unknown to me. My life became a ritual of going to spiritual healers. I felt sick but for no apparent reason. Baby Sharnell would grab her little head in her high chair and squeeze it and cry. My father, Walt, would sit next to her, trying to console her. It was awful to see your baby suffer. The dark energy was so strong in my home that I was told to put small crucifixes that were blessed by a priest throughout our home. I did just that. An evil, satanic energy would flow right through our big house from room to room. Also, it was at this time that a boy who lived about fifteen miles from us was abducted at gunpoint as he walked home with friends from a convenience store. He was never found.

Life as I had known it had become extinct. I was living a life of horror in my own home. Marc seemed confused about it as well. We were being attacked by forces so strong that I even sought out medicine men from different reservations. Now, I was learning how to make a "soul tie," a piece of colored material that is cut into a one-inch square and filled with one pinch of pipe tobacco. It is brought together at the top and tied with a red thread. These ties are made in various colors that represent the need and to what spirit you are asking for help. You must say a prayer as you hold each soul tie. The key to this whole thing is that each tie is held together on the same string. I worked on this project with several Native American women for an entire afternoon. I prayed for my situation to stop as I held each tiny pouch of tobacco of various colors. You are told to make a certain amount of red, brown, blue, yellow, and white soul ties, which are all strung on the same thread. I was directed to pray to the spirits as I touched each one. I do not remember the exact number of ties that are required by the Native American council, but the project has a definite purpose; it is similar to a prayer chain or Catholic rosary. In other words, the one making the tie is expecting positive, powerful results from the outcome of this project. You must believe in the power of Native American spirits, and I did. I had to believe in more than what my Christian religion had taught me.

I had gone to visit my neighbor lady at her home. She was the minister of a large Protestant church in our area. I told her about what I was experiencing. She simply looked at me and said, "You are experiencing mental illness. You cannot be attacked by the devil if you are a Christian and have been baptized." I immediately left her home in shame and disillusionment. Her son had played with our son. We went to the church of which she was the pastor. She became my enemy. I was embarrassed. I asked myself, "How could she have embarrassed me and humiliated me as she did?" Well, this sore feeling lasted for years to come. She finally did apologize to me. I still had a hard time accepting the apology.

Now by this time, the dark energy that attacked me every minute of my day continued. The direction from which it came from was the west. My kitchen window faced the west, and I was always in that room either cooking, baking, working at my desk, talking on the phone, or visiting friends or family at the kitchen table. I started to identify the directions from which this energy would enter my home. I was told to put a little piece of a pocket mirror on all of my windows that in turn would reflect this bad energy from coming into the house. We had over thirty windows in our home. I did just that. Then I was told to put table salt around the perimeter of our large house. Another healer directed me to bury a crystal rock one inch down into the soil for each corner of the house. I followed these directions. Then I could not sleep well with all of this stress. I was shown how to make a circle with various rocks that were laid out on a cardboard sheet under my bed. Each stone that was represented had a meaning in this energy grid. The purpose of this project was to raise the positive energy from the vibration of the rocks into the room that would thus diminish the negative vibration coming into the house from these satanic people. They concentrated on me twenty-four hours per day. Later, I was told that there were three covens working on me around the clock because I had stolen Liana from her mother.

I was the wife and mother of the home. My children could feel this energy coming from me. I was worried that everyone would disown me because of how they felt around me. Being too tired for sex didn't help my relationship with Marc either. It was I who wanted sex to obtain intimacy with Marc. He was not feeling the same exact way. Sex was more of a routine for him. He would wait for me to initiate it. However, prior to having children or even after Josh was born, Marc was sweet, intimate, and caring in our lovemaking. Sex became a Saturday night ritual after we had gone out for dinner.

He now carried all of the financial responsibility of our family of six. Since he worked on a commission basis in sales, he could never really rest. If he got depressed, it would not be uncommon to find him driving home in a new car or truck. He never consulted me about any purchase of which he made for himself. Marc was a good provider, but we lived a stressful life with the uncertainty of his income and our large expensive lifestyle. He made well over $300, 000 per year, which was thirty years ago. Without a college education, he did extremely well. He had a quick mind and business training he had obtained from his father, grandfather, and uncle. He was likeable, friendly, and political. I did not have to worry about money matters, I thought at that time. I, in turn, also had developed some profit-sharing monies from my former job that I held in a portfolio at a local bank. Marc's parents and their friends were wealthy. They vacationed as they wished to foreign countries and lived at a gated community along a golf course. Their friends were former businesspeople who were enjoying their retirement in warm climates. After Dad had retired, they lived in a condo on a golf course for some time but then moved to a larger condo. As their neighbors aged and failed, they found this to be annoying and thus moved into an upscale gated community in a beautiful home with a pool. It was here that they called home. I visited with the kids and Marc once per year. Marc went a second time alone. Eleanor loved her sons and wanted to visit Marc alone without me or the kids.

CHAPTER 20

Marc Tries to Create a "Mental Illness" State of Mind

ABOUT THIS TIME, a preteen boy was kidnapped at gunpoint from our nearby community and never found. I began to have phone calls coming into our home most of the day. Our house phone would ring, and I would answer it only to have a person on the other end sitting in silence. This would go on for about a year. I would blame it on Sue, Marc's ex-wife, who was angry that we had won custody of their daughter. I was getting worn out mentally from its constant occurrence that was day after day. It did not happen in the evening, however. At that time, we did not have "caller ID," so it was impossible to trace. If you traced it from the phone company, you would need the call to come in three times on the same number. These harassing people knew this and would always call twice and then change the number that they were calling from. I would complain to Marc, and he would simply "turn a deaf ear" to my complaints!

After we got "caller ID" numbers on our phone, which showed the caller who had just called, the puzzle was a bit easier to trace! One morning about four o'clock, I heard our house phone ring from my upstairs bedroom. Marc answered it from our master bedroom that was directly below mine. He spoke on the phone for twenty minutes. The next day, I took the liberty to dial the number that had called our home at 4:00 a.m. A kind woman answered the phone. She was willing to talk to me. I told her that someone from her household had called our home at 4:00 a.m. She knew about it. I then asked her if she had a teenage son! She replied with "No, I am an elderly lady and live with my adult soon who is in his fifties!" She told me that she had heard her son talk on the phone for twenty minutes also in the wee hours of the morning. She also said that he was very agitated and loud. I asked her what her son did for work. She stated that he was a district attorney in Dallas. Well, I thanked her for her wisdom and honesty. Now I knew that the puzzle had gotten more complex for me to figure out.

What was Marc involved in? Who were all of these different people from varied backgrounds who were calling at all hours of the day and night? Were they related somehow? It was mind-boggling. Of course I would not get anything but silence from Marc. Now, he was not yet in local politics at this time. So rule that out. However, he had gotten a judge over the weekend to sign an order to keep Liana in our household; but he had to reside in Wisconsin, not Texas.

Also, during this time, which is now twenty-seven years later, the unsolved case of the boy who was taken at gunpoint and never found near our home has come up with new DNA evidence that leads to a pedophile who still resides in the area.

My question was this: was Marc involved with a group of individuals who were in a secretive business with like members throughout the country? Did this have anything to do with the abduction at gunpoint of the boy who was never found? A large foundation was set up for missing children at this time because of the abduction.

CHAPTER 21

A Search in Our Woods

T HE HOUSE PHONE ringing up to twenty times per day with a person on the other end who would not identify himself or herself worked negatively on my mental state. Marc ignored it all. After all, he was at the office. He ignored all of it. That was odd in itself.

The missing boy disappeared in October. He was a preteen, the right age for a pedophile to be attracted to. There were witnesses, his brother and friend who were with him on his return home from a store while riding his bike near an open field. Very bad energy leaked over our community. Halloween went by, and Christmas was sad with parents who feared for their own children's safety. Doors became locked, burglar alarms were installed, and children were off the streets. Halloween parties were held in schools, and children were not allowed to go out that year.

After the boy went missing, I felt a strange "stillness" around my home. We lived in a wooded area, and I wondered if the boy could be on our property. Helicopters combed our area but did not find the boy.

In the spring, in our woods, a satanic group on motorcycles started meeting every Friday and Saturday night. Our dogs would run the perimeter of our property line and would bark all night. They were exhausted and slept during the day. I called the sheriff to check out the woods. He and Marc said it was just deer. My neighbors were complaining to me about the sound of drumming in the once-peaceful woods. I was terrified! I thought for sure that whoever had taken the boy would take one of our four children. My cleaning lady, Maggie, would pick up our little children from the bus stop while I got groceries. I had Liana carry mace in her backpack. Marc stayed aloof. He told me that I was overreacting and that our children would be untouched. I did not understand him. How could he know that?

Our house became "spiritually" haunted. The window shades would move by themselves! A voice was heard in the fireplace by my friend Roberta and myself. A visiting girlfriend could see a white cloud hanging over my head in the dining room as we ate lunch. Small gnat flies would hover over my head and become pests. This would happen anywhere I went. It was embarrassing, and who could explain it?

The group who met in our woods on these weekends continued drumming their drums until the first frost, one year after the boy went missing.

The motorcycles came into the dark woods one by one and left the same way. The last driver stayed to be the "spotter" and left several minutes after the others.

My husband's employee June and I decided to search our woods. We planned to do this in October, one year after the boy went missing. June and I walked into the area of the woods that had been cleared when we built the house. Remember the first house was built and burned down after lightning had hit the cedar shingles on Labor Day two years before. June and I went scouting into the woods, but it did not last long. She had followed a deer path that led to the north. I was scouting the perimeter of a large round opening where the tall grass had been smashed. As I looked down near my right foot, I saw a piece of red plaid material, about six inches long and five inches wide. I stooped down to pick it up. Then to my surprise, I was thrust backward by a small creature that was about three feet tall. It was a demon! He would not let me pick up the material! I was terrified and let out a shrill yell that then alarmed June. I called to her, "Run, June, run!" but not like reading my first book in grade 1! The dogs were barking at this thing, and we all ran back to the garage! Never had I seen a demon. Well, I did not go back to that spot again, but Marc did. My nanny, Vera, told me that Marc had come home from work one day to comb this area for the evidence that I had found. When I retraced my steps again but staying a distance away this time, the material had been removed! It was evidence that I was right. Humans had been there drumming into the wee hours of the morning! I had found evidence of a victim who had worn a red plaid flannel shirt that had been torn off him or her. Marc had lied to me and the sheriff! Was Marc involved with this group? Did he give them permission to meet on our land for a whole summer and autumn?

CHAPTER 22

The Killer Calls

I T IS A new day. I am trying to recover from the fear I had felt in our woods only yesterday. June and I had run from the woods after I had been thrust backward from a demon who was protecting the property that had been claimed as a satanic ritual site. I never got to touch or pick up the red plaid material that would have fit into my hand as evidence that someone had been hurt or killed in our woods.

The children are off to school, and my phone is ringing. I ask myself, "Should I even pick it up? Will it be another person stalking me by calling and not speaking?" I answer the phone. I gingerly pick up the receiver to hear a man say, "Satin."

Let me tell you what I saw and felt. First of all, just the fear I felt from the man at the other end of the phone immediately made my hand shake. I held the phone a foot away from my ear. I had never felt a man as "evil" as this person. At that time, I did not know that I was "intuitive." I did not understand that I could see, hear, taste, and feel spiritually. Let me tell you what I saw when I heard this man's voice.

First of all, I removed the receiver away from my head. My hand shook with traumatizing fear. I did not elect to speak. I saw the color "red," which means very bad. In the Native American religion and spiritually, it is the worst color to see in your mind. It means blood shedding in a "not-so-good way." It is not the same as being killed in war as a soldier who had a destination or purpose. The "red" was all I saw when I shut my eyes to view my mind.

I was totally silent as if to let the "assailant" think that I was not there even though he knew I was. In a split second, the "red blood color" disappeared, and yet another scene was presented to me. I could visualize there was water to the left of this area that had long dry grass. The terrain was on a gradual slope with only an isolated tree. I was looking at the lifeless body of a preteen boy who was lying on his stomach. He was clothed in blue jeans and tennis shoes. His right arm was lying above his head and curved over the top of his head. The right side of his face was pressed against the tall dry grass. About six feet and to the right of his body stood a very alive man. He wore stovepipe jeans that were denim blue, and his legs looked tall and slim. He wore work boots that were tan in color with leather laces that went to his ankles. He would not allow me to see any more of him than what I mentioned.

I had never met neither the killer nor the victim. Within seconds of getting these images from the man on the other end of the receiver, my still-shaking hand laid down the receiver carefully, without my saying a word. Now I was more than terrified. I did not know who or where this man was who wanted to show me this scene. I could not correlate how I was targeted to get these continuous phone calls of harassment and now to have received a "psychically visual" view but silent message from the killer. I asked myself, "Is Marc, my husband, involved in this satanic cult?" Did he have something to do with the disappearance of this preteen boy by association? To this day, as I write this book, this child is still considered missing. There is a silence in the county where this abduction took place, and no person dared to come forth with any information for fear of disappearing themselves.

CHAPTER 23

Marc Abuses Me Verbally and Mentally

W HEN I WOULD relay these strange occurrences to my husband, they seemed to be ignored. Really they were not. It was then that Marc decided to do various things to me that I did not learn about until twenty-six years later. As I went to work to unlock the mysteries that were taking place on our property and to me, Marc reciprocated by his "wrongdoings" of "masterminding" my mind by trying to make me look "delusional" and therefore not respected or reputable. We were divided as a couple. Keep in mind, I had two small children and his two teenagers to raise at this time.

I would be exhausted after waking in the morning. Never was I rested. I slept with Marc at this time. My insides did not feel warm and fuzzy or secure with Marc. My love came from my children. I was alone except for my mother friend, Vera, and her husband, Carl. I talked to Vera several times during the day. She was our nanny should we take a trip. Carl was her husband. He groomed our lawn. Together, they were like parents to me.

The more information I came upon, Marc remained aloof. He denied the "missing boy's" fate. Our whole community lived in fear. Marc said to me that I should stop worrying about OUR kids because nothing would happen to them. It was as if he knew something I did not. It was like we were a protected family or something.

All sorts of weird things began to happen to me. I would hear a continuous song playing over and over in my head during the day. I did not listen to the radio but rather had the TV on. Marc was missing emotionally. Actually he was sharing his emotions with his bookkeeper, Sandy, who worked alone with him for ten years. I could feel someone trying to pound nails into my head. My arms and legs itched. Small gnats would appear and fly around my head should I meet a friend for coffee. I tried to find diversions to get myself away from Marc and this dirty energy he carried.

I got a job as a social worker in another town, but I was so consumed with all of this that I came late to work because I felt drugged and could not wake up, leaving me groggy until I drank more than enough coffee. I did not suspect my husband of anything yet. I was looking for "outsiders" who were actually Marc's satanic friends, including Sandy at his office, she being the woman he refused to replace at this time.

Marc's friend ran a large department at the hospital. I went there for tests because of all of these sensations I was feeling. I now was Marc's victim. At the same time, all of my daily duties did not change. He was in the cult, and so was Sandy. The closer I got to finding out what happened to the missing boy and the connection Marc had to all of it, the more heightened the abuse I received from Marc and his involvement.

Vera tipped me off by telling me that she found a tape recorder under our master bed. Marc had been playing the same song over and over as he had apparently drugged me while I slumbered. Every morning a small car with a loud muffler would scurry along our long and winding driveway in the woods and turn around in the circular driveway. There was a computer screen near the dashboard of this car. I was left alone with negative feelings from Marc and all of whom he associated with. After this car would surface only feet from my bedroom window, my physical symptoms would seem to worsen and last all day. They included terrible headaches and nausea. Marc denied hearing the car each morning for months. I did not suspect my husband of his involvement; how naive was I. Remember I was taught to trust! All of this happened after the boy went missing from our community.

CHAPTER 24

Mother-in-Law

M Y MOTHER-IN-LAW, ELEANOR, and father-in-law, Andes, went to visit my parents. My family lived in a basement house that had the front open to a lake. It was like living at a summer cottage. I liked it. Eleanor liked my parents very much because she was as evil as my own mother. My dad liked to keep the peace unless they "screwed him over." My father-in-law, Andes, was intelligent, shrewd, and experienced in the business world. He had a meek and humble spirit the whole time I had known him. I loved this man and took my conversations to him rather to her, the witch. At one point, when they were very old, he had said to me, "Satin, there are days that I would like to kill her." He really meant it, and I knew just what he was trying to tell me.

Eleanor would at times be glad that I was taking over the job of caring for her favorite grandson. She welcomed new babies but said she didn't want any more grandchildren. She looked at this whole situation as a challenge, which was "How will I get these young ones into the synagogue?" She would say to me, "Oh, such a beautiful girl, if only I could get you to join our sisterhood." I thought she had meant the Jewish women's group, but in essence she meant her coven. Then I started to wonder who was in her Jewish sisterhood. Was my sister-in-law or her mother in it? Were all of the Jewish women Eleanor was friends with in this? It was always a puzzle. I also wondered what I would benefit if I ever joined it. Well, after watching Eleanor's behavior, I would never join anything that she was associated with. Sharing her son was plenty for me. Marc would always say that she thought that she was a pea in the pod that Marc and I shared as a married couple.

My sister-in-law Rachael, whom we called Rae, had plenty to say about Eleanor. She was even Jewish and had a lot of trouble with Mom. At many points, Charlie, Eleanor's oldest living son, was torn between his mother and his wife. I would just observe. Rae and Charlie had left Milwaukee to live in California. They moved with the thought that life would be better for them there. It was a disaster. Rae even left Charlie there and moved back to Milwaukee. Eleanor called me one day saying that she and Dad wanted their married son Charlie to stay with them in California and wanted Rae, his wife, to stay in Milwaukee. She was asking me to support her sick decision of creating a divorce. I told Marc about it and that I was not going to help her create a divorce between his brother and his brother's wife. He took care of it.

Now that I knew how Eleanor manipulated situations, I was very cautious of any dealings with her. Rae did not trust me because Eleanor was trying to keep me on her side of the fence. This woman was a tyrant. She lived to cause trouble. There were two sides to her personality. She told me that she created her own world to live in and believe. She had beady brown eyes, and when she got mad, it felt like she had slit your throat. The kitchen is where all conversation took place. She would have me buy her ingredients, and preparing the meal would take up her entire afternoon. Her ears would be listening to every word within walking distance. She was a radar magnet.

On the good side, she would knit baby hats for newborn babies in their local hospital. She also had her favorites in grandchildren. Her firstborn granddaughter had passed away when she was younger than five. An illness that is now treated successfully took her young life. So she doted on the second-born granddaughter, the child of Charlie and Rae. Next, her favorite grandchild was my stepson, Jake. From then on, favoritism depended on who would snitch on a parent or relative to tell her something. She loved to talk to grandchildren as they always bore their soul to her and thought that they were doing a good deed. She would reward the innocent snitches with money. As they got older, these children learned this same trait. She really played on the stepfamily unit or Charlie and Rae's marriage. When I look back at pictures of Marc, me, and her, she would make a sour face to show her disapproval of Marc's choice.

CHAPTER 25

More on Grandma Eleanor

MARC HIMSELF REMINDED me of a mobster. He could be a big bully or loving and kind, giving one the impression of a big teddy bear. His mother was the queen of witchcraft. Her eyes would shift from normal brown eyes to beady, devious small eyes. The combination of both personalities seen in both mother and son was hard to describe. His mother was vicious and cruel, especially to me. Her friends gave me pity.

My in-laws had a lot of money. I call it old money. This is money that was either passed down to them through inheritance or had been with them for a long time. It was with them a long time. Dad had worked in his business a long time with his cousin. The two of them had made quite a name for themselves and had made an industrial impact on our community over a long period.

I had joined the women of this mob. The family operated on a political basis, not a loving atmosphere. That was for sure. What I mean by political was you were used and gossiped about. You did what they wanted you to do in order to get their inheritance after they were dead and gone. Later in life, Grandma would ask me if I liked my stepson's girlfriend. If I said no, she would see to it that she would be gone. My former step-daughter-in-law reported to me that she had a terrifying dream before marrying Grandma's favorite grandson. She remarked that she had a dream that her wedding dress simply shredded into pieces and fell to the floor, leaving her naked just prior to walking down the aisle with Jake. I was not surprised.

If Eleanor liked you, which was highly unlikely for being her son's wife, you might have a fighting chance. I mean the fight was still a cockfight. What I realized after many years was that if you would not do the dirty work that she asked you to do on her behalf, she absolutely had no need for you. So either you confided in her, snitched on other family members to feed her evil appetite or she would give you a run for your money. Marc loved his father and mother but tolerated his mother. I was not welcomed at their home other than being the mother and stepmother of the children. This made it hard for everyone because we were not all on the same page. The grandchildren would know my feelings and snitch on their own mother to be on the good side of Grandma.

I, on one occasion, referred to her as an asshole, which I am not proud of; but if you knew her intended evil on us, you would completely understand. Little Josh, who was only three years old, grabbed the phone from his sister and said, "Mom says that you are an asshole." Liana instantly covered the receiver. The only good thing about this occurrence was that Josh had a speech impairment, and she could not distinctly hear his words. I was saved by a speech impairment.

After her visits, we would all get the flu. Or I would have to search our large house for items she would bring in her purse and plant each one in various places throughout the 6,200-plus-square-foot home. These items were intended to do harm to me. It was witchcraft. I call it real witchcraft. It worked, and I would pee foam from a eucalyptus leaf from our house plant that she would put somewhere in the house.

Instead of looking for Easter eggs, I searched for feathers. On one occasion, Sharnell called me upstairs to tell me that Grandma had put a feather on her bathroom countertop. To add to the witchcraft recipe, she had wrapped five strands of Sharnell's hair around the feather. She included one of her gray hair. I frantically looked for phone numbers of any Native American medicine men to ask what I should do with it so it would not hurt Sharnell. Now, looking for that type of resource is not found in the Yellow Pages. I must say, I was desperate and resourceful in finding help with the experts in this field of study. I then learned to look for objects that were hidden in my own home with the intention to do me bodily harm.

I secured help once again through a Native American tribe in my regional area. I was told to wrap the feather in tissue and not to look back as I burn it outside of our once-peaceful home prior to Eleanor and Andes's visit. I did just that. Instantly, I questioned myself if it would be necessary to unwrap and discard the hair prior to burning it so Sharnell would not feel a burning sensation in her body from my burning of the feather. Needless to say, it was mind-boggling. This went on for years. I had to quickly learn a solution for each prank she pulled. She had been a witch since she was nineteen years of age. It was her coven she would often request I join. She would comment that I would make a good sister in her sisterhood. I refused and remained a recipient of her attacks until Marc refused her entrance into our home for the next ten years. I hate to give her credit for evil deeds, but she was darn good at this game. Her devious actions were terrifying, dangerous, exhausting, and painful, not to mention consuming of one's mind and emotions.

Marc had free rein of his own life during our marriage since I was so preoccupied with situations as I just described. One visit came to a finale, and I would fear the next visit. My friends stuck with me no matter what happened or what I told them. Maybe they were amused. They stayed with me for the duration of my twenty-five-year marriage and are still here.

CHAPTER 26

Whatever Happened to Aunt Neena?

N EENA WAS MARC'S adopted sister. She was adopted at only two years old. I really liked her, and we visited each time she came to stay at our home. She confided in me about how her life had played out. It was what I expected; her own mother was jealous of her and tried the "control" game with her as well. If she did not please her mother, she too got the "evil" end of things. Andes, I called him Dad, simply because I had a special bond with him, loved Neena and was her dad. As he showed his daughter attention, of course, Eleanor would get jealous and show her evil side to Neena.

Her story unfolded to me as she sat at the end of my farmhouse-style kitchen table on a cold, rainy day in April. I had met Neena after she reappeared to the family after eight years in hiding from them shortly after I married her brother, Marc.

She trusted me enough to tell her story. I was not surprised to know the truth about her mysterious disappearance. She left her home state of Wisconsin to drive herself alone to Los Angeles, California, many years ago. The reason? Her mother had threatened her that if she should leave her husband, La Chino, an arrangement would be made for her own mother and two brothers to admit her to a mental facility. She was only twenty-two years old. With no money or formal schooling and knowing no one there, nor along the way, she left her spouse and three-year-old son to save herself from the depicted doom that would befall her should she proceed with her desire to divorce her husband, La Chino. La Chino was not a bad husband. She was not in love or had ever been. It was sort of an arranged marriage in the fact that the young man she was interested in was not accepted by the family because he was the wrong religion. La Chino, on the other hand, was the same religion and well-liked by both of her parents. Besides, he got along well with Eleanor, and they shared many conversations about Neena.

Neena was depressed, scared, and angry and felt pushed to the corner. Again, her life was controlled by her mother. Now, the threat of being put away had been set before her, should she not succumb to her mother's wishes for her life. Her mother told her that she was not capable of being a mother and that someone else should raise little Andre.

It was getting close to the time she was to pick up Andre from his day care provider. Feeling so worthless and alone, she decided that her mother, Eleanor, had to be right. She was not worthy of being little Andre's mother. With despair in her heart, Neena told me how she left Andre with the sitter, and she drove away alone, abandoning her young son, spouse, and family. I came to her as she cried, reliving that terrible moment that changed her life and theirs. It was the guilt from Eleanor, her adopted mother, that drove her into desperation. She departed in the night, alone, dangerously, to escape asylum instead of getting a divorce and a split custody arrangement to raise little Andre. She was on the run with only a car and enough cash to survive a couple of weeks. My spirit knew that Eleanor was behind this tragedy. Of course, Neena was to blame. Neena survived and stayed away from the family for eight years. Finally, she decided to return and called her brother Charlie to pick her up at the airport exactly eight years later. It was then that I came into the family to meet Neena.

Eleanor accepted the return of Neena after the family had hired private investigators without results. She stayed in their home and was supported by them once again. Unfortunately, the wrath of her mother was not yet complete. There was a plan yet to unfold.

CHAPTER 27

My Dad's Death

I HAD MET ANN, my mother's new friend, when I was five years old. My relationship with her lasted until my parents had celebrated their fiftieth wedding anniversary. Ann was writing to me prior to the special event, as she had planned to surprise them and fly over the Atlantic to be with us for the event. Mom was secretly suffering from dementia. My father was covering for her illness. It was a family trait to always try to cover up anything that was not quite right. What we didn't know was that Dad had bladder cancer that had spread throughout his whole body. He was keeping his problem to himself and did not go to the doctor until Mother called me one day, saying that Dad was lying on the floor trying to breathe. At this point, he was her caretaker dealing with her dementia. She would not eat until he would come home from work and would then take her out to eat dinner.

My sister-in-law, who was an RN, had suspected that Dad had cancer but did not want to say anything. I had noticed on my monthly visits home that the house was not clean, as it had always been. Dad's shirts smelled like Dad. They did not seem freshly washed or pressed as Mom had done them over all of their married years together. I noticed that all of the kitchen drawers were neat and tidy. Mom had forgotten how to fry an egg. Life was getting hectic for them in their secret life together.

One day, Mom called me to say that Dad had come home early to lie down and take a nap. She thought that he had died. Her intuition was only off three weeks from the truth. I lived an hour away at that time, and she wanted me to come over and check if Dad had died during his nap. I told her to call 911. She said that I had to do that and drive over. I told her to shake him. She did, and he woke up to say he was alive. Each day was similar to this until it got worse. I called my brother Brett. It took days of convincing Dad that he needed to be seen by a doctor. After the first visit to the small hospital, Dad was diagnosed with bladder cancer that had spread to his lungs and had less than three months to live. He was okay with this bad news as taking care of Mom had worn him to a frazzle. We were not all right with this deal. Dad was only seventy and had been enjoying his life playing in a polka band as a drummer. He was a grandparent to our sons and daughters, a dad, a husband, a caretaker, a provider, and the glue that held our family together.

When Mom heard the news that he was going to die very soon, she was very angry with him.

After all, he was going to leave her. He had always taken care of her. She never worked outside of the house and only had two children who were eleven years apart. I think she planned it that way.

Dad thought he could peacefully die in his own house. He sat in his chair by the TV and decided to share this news to his family and friends. They flocked to the homestead to visit and share old stories from the past. Marc and I took turns going there as we had quite an active life with kids, his work, and life. Brother Brett came daily with a cooler full of fresh food that went untouched. Mom would not eat unless Dad would. Dad did not have an appetite. Brett's friend owned a local restaurant and willingly offered to supply a meal free each day for them, hand delivered from three miles away. They refused all welfare or county assistance. Since I had a degree in social work, I had become the enemy. I was not in denial about this situation at all. Brett was bringing vitamins and health food supplements to the house and sitting up late with Dad, discussing this natural cure for his cancer. It was amazing and sad at the same time.

Each day Dad's condition had noticeably worsened. He was so weak that Brett had to escort him to the bathroom and give him a shower with Dad sitting on a chair. Then Brett started negotiating with Dad about how he should get ten thousand dollars more than me because he had helped out a lot. The timing of financial negotiation was disgusting. I was just the daughter who had had all of the family dinners and brought grandchildren into the picture. Dad stuck to his guns and gave us both fifty thousand dollars each. He was always fair that way. Remember, it seemed that I was well-off financially.

Each day Dad slumped down in his chair. His ankles were waterlogged. His lungs were now filling up with fluid, and he was going to drown in his own fluid. We had to do something. Brett argued with Marc and me, saying that Dad had wished to die at home. I was not there the night Marc had come home to me saying, "You have to do something, Satin. Your brother will not let me call 911, and your dad will not make it through the night." Lily, Brett's wife, had gone home to get up for work the next day. She did not insist on Dad going to the ER either. So I called the county nurse who then called an ambulance. Dad barely made it alive to the hospital. He was drowning.

Dad enjoyed his next week visiting with more friends and family with the fine care the hospital provided. Something unusual happened, though. Dad got very nervous one day and told me to take Mom to my house. He did not want her at the hospital. He demanded she leave. We found out later that he had a girlfriend who worked at the bank in a small town only twenty miles from my hometown. What a shock that was. She came with another woman friend from the bank to see Dad for the last time. He was having an affair. Sources said it had begun four years earlier. So when Mom was losing her mind and calling Brett with the news that Dad was cheating on her, she was right. I believed her all along. I had said to Brett, "Maybe Mom is right about this." His response was "Well, wouldn't you cheat if you were him?"

To make this long story short, as I always say, Dad spent only three weeks preparing to meet his Maker. I gave him a big hug in the hospital and told him that I loved him. He waited until we were all together in the nursing home before he passed away. That morning, he had asked if I was going to come. He waited for me. Brett and Lily, as well as our son Josh, his best buddy, were by his side. I never liked these things, so I slid into the kitchen of the home to make myself a piece of toast. That is exactly what Dad used to do: slide away from the situation and refer to food for comfort. It was a family diversion trait he passed on to me. My mother stood at the end of his bed as he died, eating an oatmeal cookie and sipping on a cup of coffee. Lily, being the nurse of the family, talked to Dad to the end. Brett gave Dad the "go-ahead" to die. Lily, Marc, and Brett went into the chapel and sobbed relentlessly. Tears clung to the chapel floor just as the tears had clung to the tile floor in my parents' bedroom when my mother broke the news to my dad that his own mother had passed away some thirty-five earlier.

Remember, I was taught not to show emotion from my mother at an early age. I did not shed one tear. It wasn't until February, the month of my birth, that I simply broke down and cried at my kitchen table, which I considered the most important place in any home. Dad's stepgrandchildren were not at the funeral but called while he was in the hospital. They were with their mother out of state.

Marc had suggested that we have balloons representing each of our four children attached to an array of flowers next to the casket. After the funeral, we drove home on the most beautiful sunny day. One of the kids opened up the backseat window to witness the balloon marked "Grandpa" sneak out of the window frame and gracefully drift into the heavens from our moving car. What a message that was for all of us. I had a feeling that Dad had some negotiating to do with his Maker before he entered the pearly gates. I had witnessed him gripping a wet towel in his tight fists, and he was very angry with God for not sparing his life when he knew he was physically doomed, only a day before he died.

After he had passed away, I witnessed his presence spiritually with different scents in the house or visual sightings throughout the home or at the lake. Since I can see, hear, touch, feel, and sense spirits, I was very aware of his presence. As I drove my mother back to her new apartment one warm sunny day in the midsummer, I actually saw Dad standing with his arm up, leaning against a tree along the side of the highway. He was waiting for me to see him with a big smile on his face.

CHAPTER 28

Marc's Physical Abuse Begins

I FINALLY WENT TO see a counselor. I went to see a man named Juan, not my old boyfriend who ended up to be a clinical psychologist but rather someone whom the family had known for a long time. As I told him about Sue joining an occult movement after we had obtained custody of Liana, he cringed in his seat. The dark energy coming at me was so strong that he actually shifted his own body to its side to avoid it from entering him. It was not long into the conversation that he suggested that I go on a medication that would block this power from entering me. I was allergic to most drugs and feared that I would have an allergic reaction to anything he had suggested. He thought I should go into the hospital psychiatric unit for one week to start a medication and adjust to it without feeling afraid about my throat closing with an allergic reaction. I agreed to do just that. Marc even called Sue and asked her just what the hell she was up to. She, of course, denied anything of the sort of wishing us ill will after we had "stolen" her daughter.

There I was in the hospital, right where Marc really wanted me. I went in voluntarily and could go out the same way. Dr. Volerna, a woman from Hungary, was wonderful. She found a drug that worked to block this strange phenomenon that was coming to me or at me. She knew what it was and called it a "bunch of shit." She was a small young woman with a power and sense about her that I truly respected. She had worked with this type of thing before in another city.

As I lay in the hospital room overlooking the roof of the hospital, I awoke at 5:00 a.m. to feel a strong presence of a person standing next to my right shoulder. I looked over my side to see not at all what I had expected. I was looking for a nurse just checking in on me, but instead, I saw a small girl about five years old simply standing at my right side. I stared at her. She had long eyelashes. Her hair was shoulder length and medium brown. The dress was brown with small polka dots in the material. It had a large white collar with lace around it. She wore white tights and black patent leather shoes with a bow. Now that I think of it, she resembled my aunt Harriet, who had died at four years old from diphtheria. Her picture hung in the kitchen of my grandparents' farm home. They explained to me at a very early age just who she was. I felt a very good but strange power of strength coming from this little girl. As I looked at her, I noticed that her eyes were wide open and they never blinked. Was I seeing an angel? Yes, I was indeed in the presence of a true creature of Christ. This was an angel who was sent to me from heaven to give me spiritual strength.

When I was four years old, I had seen a lion lying by my bedroom dresser in my upstairs bedroom. I distinctly remember telling my mother what I had seen and had asked her if she could see him. Then she told me about the lion and the lamb story. She could not see the lion but did tell me that he was protecting me while I slept.

The pastor from our church came to visit me. She herself was the one who said that I was mentally ill. I did not appreciate her visit and requested a Catholic priest to visit instead. He was completely different in style, speech, and respect in regard to me and my strange situation. I remember that my husband had told me that he had served Sue divorce papers while she was in the same unit. I did not correlate the two being similar, however.

In all of my life, I had never before been on any medication or needed a psychiatrist, but now this family was different. Both my husband and my mother-in-law wanted me to be on a psychotropic drug. My father and brother came to the hospital to see what this was all about. They did not trust Marc. They were suspicious of this whole event since he had had the same situation occur with his first wife. I was too befuddled to know just what was going on. There were nurses and other people up there. I knew I did not fit in with them. I felt like I was in prison even though I could have just walked out at any time. Marc did not come to see me. That was very odd. Matter of fact, he tried to keep me there without my consent for two weeks. The doctor and psychologist were now very suspicious of Marc and his intention to keep me in the hospital. They did not trust him and told me about the situation. My father and brother also knew that Marc was up to something. He was. We did not know what the purpose was. Now I do. He was trying to make a "delusional" file on me in the hospital, in other words, give me a history of psychological problems like he did his former wife, Sue. That gave him an edge in a custody fight over his children. Now he would create the same pattern with me. It had worked with her, and he wanted to repeat the style and format used by him and his mother in the past.

The doctor knew this as well. She thought he was creating my problem somehow and began to think that he was involved in a satanic occult. She had worked with this in another clinic. She had to be very careful as to how to handle him to avoid a lawsuit. I left after a week and made it clear to him that I was told by the staff that he was trying to keep me there for another week. A nurse spilled her guts to me by saying, "You don't know what you are in here for, girl?" I replied no. She said, "Your chart says that you are 'delusional.'" Now, I felt betrayed by my doctor and knew that was not the case. I did not know whom to trust. I noticed that my mother did not come to see me, but rather, two of my closest women friends did visit. They were Nan and Marcella. These two women were my true friends for over thirty years now. They still are friends. No questions asked. They came and supported me.

I came home and went about my business. Marc would make fun of me and say, "Just pop a pill. It's easy, Satin." Then he would imitate putting a fake pill into his mouth. When I think of what a total ass he was, his karma thickens. He told everyone in his path that I was suffering from "delusions." Really, I was not. With this new drug, the problem was solved, but I gained weight, a lot of it. My foxy figure was no longer intact. He was a new diabetic too. He had a big bag of syringes next to his side of our bed in his dresser. I never really suspected that he would ever harm me, although I kept saying to myself that I was really lucky that I was not married to a medical doctor because they could inject a person while they slept.

I was very busy raising kids now, all four of them. I started to feel "spacey" in the morning when I woke up. I drank a lot of coffee to overcome this feeling. The coffee made me jittery even with this medication. Also, I awoke with bruises on my hands or on my breasts. When I had my yearly Pap smear and uterus exam with the mammogram, my breast tissue was not normal. The physician could not figure out why the tissue had been broken or stabbed into somehow. They wanted to put a metal marker in that area to watch for cancer. I refused. It was a mystery. There was one mystery after another with my body.

One morning my chest hurt so badly that I could hardly breathe. My head hurt. It felt like it was going to explode. Then I started to feel something in my head. It hurt badly, as if fishhooks had been put in my head. That sounds really crazy, but all of this came into my full knowledge at a later date. I continued to visit spiritual healers. They would take these "spiritual objects" out of my head. My healer would have me repeat a mantra over and over for my own power to take over. She also instructed me how to call her in that fashion if I was under a "spiritual warfare" that I could not handle myself. The psychiatrist had told me that only 3 percent of the population is attacked by a satanic cult. I was one of them. No wonder most people thought I was crazy since they had never heard of such a thing.

During one of my healing sessions, Bet had decoded me from Satan. She said that since this was a Satanist group that was attacking me, this would help. Well, to my surprise, when my son Josh and I walked into our kitchen, Josh got a satanic hook in his foot. He hurt badly, and I returned to her with him to have her remove this spiritual object from his foot. Each time, the fee was $100. I spent thousands of dollars over the years, and Marc never once complained about this. Our family could have been going on expensive vacations during these years with the money that I would have saved.

During this time, I would sprinkle our rooms with holy water. It was blessed by a Catholic priest. I also put small crucifixes in each room of the large house. The local priest would come out to bless the house and beg me to go back to the Catholic Church. I was relying on my Catholic faith. When Eleanor visited around Easter and Passover season, I had mentioned to her that I felt men in my gut or abdomen. She replied very strangely, saying, "You are a very bright girl, and one of these days, you will figure all of this out." Now, I was really on a trail to find explanations for all of this. First I was "delusional," then "a very bright girl." I was like a hound dog on a hunt for the truth.

These strange attacks continued. I, however, was on a drug that helped me but was not a cure. The gums of my mouth felt like a needle had gone through them. After this happened while I slept, I found that I needed many crowns in my mouth. I suffered so many infections that I became allergic to most antibiotics. I suffered from colitis in my rectum from nervous stress. I did not sleep rested. Waking up tired and worn out was normal. One morning, semen ran out of my uterus when I had not had sex. I totally freaked out as I sat on the toilet draining myself from who or whom or what. Marc and I had not had sex, nor had I had intercourse with anyone else. I felt alone with my strange findings. I did not want to own them. Being different from everyone else was not fun.

Liana came to me at the onset of her seventh-grade school year, saying, "Mom, something weird is happening to me." She had explained to me that she could not move her body each morning until the sun would come into her bedroom window. She told me not to tell Dad. I did, and I should not have. He cornered her against the laundry room wall with his big arms spread out and his hands on the wall next to her head, screaming at the top of his big lungs these exact words: "If I ever hear any of this again from you, I will put you in a mental institution for the rest of your life. Do you understand?" She just shook and was scared and shocked. She felt that I had betrayed her. I wanted to help her and thought he would support my understanding her position. Rather, he was covering something up that we knew nothing about.

I also had a suspicion that he was going up to her room after I had gone to bed. He never went upstairs to see the kids. After a trip, he could be home three days before he would see or talk to the children. I would have to ask him to check on the kids; he would respond with "I will see them sometime tomorrow." This was crazy. Liana never confided in me ever again. I lost all of her respect and confidence. He wanted her isolated from me in our home. If we talked too much, we may figure out not only these strange happenings in our home but also what was causing our other symptoms that were health related.

She would routinely come home on the bus, eat out of the snack drawer, and go to her room. Never did she confide in me again. Evil entered from time to time. Once I said to her that she was not acting like herself. All of a sudden a demon spoke through her, saying, "Well, Satin, if you think I need help, then help me." I was so terrified that I ran out of her room. We had been so close for so long, but now every phrase spoken between us was evaluated. Her alarm would be set for five o'clock in the morning when she got up to study. She would eat cereal and leave for school. I do not remember if she got lunch money. Marc liked this distance. United we'd fare well, and that was a threat to him. He attended all of the school conferences because he was in the public eye. Education was important because he told each child that he would never support any of them. That was extremely fearful to hear at an early age.

Jake was sent to Germany to go to high school for his junior year. He got away from the drama. Liana acted like a victim. She was invited to join Job's Daughters, and then we decided that working out of the home would be more beneficial. To our surprise, we had a difficult time getting her out of the organization. She had told them that we were abusing her. Maybe she thought that I was in on these weird things happening to her. In fact, I was a victim too. She trusted only one girl, her best friend, Bethany. I am truly sorry, dear Liana. I love you still for what you suffered in our home. I too was on a search for the "truth" of these strange happenings. From this time, Liana was estranged from me.

I hired a babysitter on Saturday nights to come into our home so she could babysit out of the house. There she befriended another family in our neighborhood. That was good. She told them she was abused. She would ignore us and the family and spend her time in her room. I did not understand her telling me that she could not move her body until the sun came into her room. Then she could move her body. She was terrified. I should have asked her more about it without her father knowing of her confiding in me. I never once thought that Marc was going up to her room and doing something to her. Was he injecting her with a drug in which she could not move her body? Was this a nerve gas drug? Why would Marc do this to his own daughter, his own flesh and blood?

Marc would always tell our two kids that they had Walsh blood running in their veins. Then he would say that his older kids had Silverstein blood in them. He would say the older kids were smarter than the younger two. Our son Josh developed a low self-esteem. Marc would actually tell him that he would not amount to much. His older two children would be praised for honor roll participation even though they were ten and thirteen years older than the younger children.

CHAPTER 29

Strange Physical Marks Appear on My Body

NOW AT THIS time, I would wake up feeling tired, completely worn out, and alone. The gums of my mouth felt like a needle had gone through them on one side. I would run to the dentist. I also suffered from many infections and would need so many antibiotics that I became allergic to most of them.

About this time, Marc wanted to visit a business client and his wife in Corpus Christi. We were just about ready to leave, but the day before, I was cleaning with a small vacuum under the big island in our kitchen. Little Sharnell had gotten into a bottom drawer and was breaking glass casserole dishes. I did not clear the countertop and jumped up with my full body weight under the ledge of the counter to protect her. Well, I did not clear the ledge of the countertop and hit my head so hard that I had compressed my neck and suffered nerve damage in my head for over six months. I doctored for this period and was worried that the strange feelings in my head would continue for my entire life. Feeling like worms were crawling in just half of my head was horrible. Marc would run me down to the U of Milwaukee Hospital to find a cure for this awful feeling. I was then directed to two different physicians, but it was not until I met the third specialist that I found an explanation for this horrible feeling.

Also, I had a spheroid sinus infection that was not treated with the right antibiotics. The fluid in my sinuses was so infected that I felt like my head was swelling. I kept doctoring to find a cure for this strange situation. Marc was never concerned. Also, I still felt like I had fishhooks in my head. I sought spiritual healers to remove them. One healer saw what was happening and just gave me a big hug. She shook her head in sympathy. I did not understand what was going on.

Here I was a mother and wife of four children and was suffering each and every day from something I did not comprehend for many years to come. I spent thousands on spiritual healers over a twenty-year period. Marc never said a thing about it either. I was totally sidetracked to what was really going on with him and this weird activity.

I woke up in the morning feeling drugged and tired. Sometimes I talked very fast as if I was on speed or meth. When I drank coffee, my condition worsened. My new psychiatrist suspected Marc in playing a big role with my strange changing condition. I was too drugged and busy to even begin to figure this strange stuff out.

I would wake up in the morning finding a bruise on my chest and could hardly move or breathe. My right hand would have a big bruise on the top of it, but I could not remember hurting it. The Mental Health Unit said that I was doing this to myself. My most common statement was that I would go to bed fine and wake up with a large bruise on my hand, chest, or breast. My legs were full of veins on the surface that I never had before.

On several occasions, I awoke in the morning with very tight indentations around my ankles, wrists, and throat. They hurt and would stay for twenty-four hours. It was as if I had been tied to a bed while I slept. Or I woke up with large scratch marks on the right side of my back that stretched from my right shoulder to below my waist. It was as if someone had taken a coin and dipped it in a burning solution and then rubbed it repeatedly crisscross down my back. My back burned for over seven days. I showed Marc. He did not want to look at this condition that had happened during my sleeping hours of the night in our marital bed. I would say, "Marc, look at my back." He would glance quickly and then always say, "Shit happens, Satin. Count your blessings." Then he would list what he thought my material blessings were. He would go on and on about how I lived in a million-dollar house, drove a Lincoln, was financially supported, and had him and the family that he had given me. My girlfriend took pictures of my back, and I would stand in a mirror and take pictures of my breasts and hand with the bruises that would appear the morning after I slept.

I also had deep indentations of a chastity belt that was used to protect young daughters from being raped. These indentations again lasted twenty-four hours. Each day I was a victim to whom? Marc would tell me that spirits were bothering me. Another episode with my back presented itself with a burning sensation over my entire upper back. It was red as though I had been sunburned severely.

Puncture wounds appeared in the palms of both of my hands, and a liquid was injected into the base of each of my fingers. Each pocket burned. Again, I would tell Marc, and he would just walk away and tell me to count my blessings. I would urinate white foam, and my feces was green in color. I would get so upset just imagining that either I would get deathly sick or I would die, leaving my small children motherless and my stepchildren to be raised by their dad who was aloof and stingy with money. The big kids always came to me for money. Marc would not give them any spending money and required that they go to work for it. Young Sharnell was already working at the age of fourteen for life. Marc had arranged with his friend to give her a job.

Marc would not give the big kids any warning to their financial independence either. As they would need something, he would just say, "Get out and get a job." There they stood without any spending money, and I would always give them cash or a credit card. Marc screamed and threatened each of us on a whim. When our young children were growing, he would grab their heads and violently shake them. I called a county social worker to report this child abuse. I would wake up from sleep only to find my head and neck aching too.

I would wake up in such pain and distress that I had to have been tortured while I slept. It was a mystery. I would retire for the night either in our master bed or in my bedroom upstairs every night. I would awaken with a big green bruise on my right hand that covered the whole hand. Or I would be bruised by what looked like the size of a fist. It would hurt so bad when I made my morning coffee that I could hardly stand the pain. I would go to our local mental health center and show them the markings on my body and the bruises as well. The psychiatrist would again say that I had done this to myself or that it was just a mere mystery. I got absolutely no help whatsoever. My report read that I was experiencing delusions. I knew that I did not do this to myself, and Marc just kept telling me that it had to be done spiritually by some unknown force. His other explanation of this situation would be that I must have a dermatology problem and that I should just count the many blessings that God had bestowed on me by giving me him. He had supplied my big house and had given me a great family, except for his mother, of course.

One morning I came out of the master shower and went into our large walk-in closet to find my yellow terry cloth robe. I dressed as usual but noticed as I put the robe over my right breast that a hole had been precisely cut out of the robe, exactly measured to fit the size of my right breast. There I stood with my right breast sticking out of the robe. I freaked out and ran to call my friends with the news on what had happened to me. They listened intently as usual to my strange details of these mysterious events that occurred each day or week. This would preoccupy my time as it was intended to do. It was actually intended to preoccupy my mind so I would not look into just what my husband found entertaining. The situation was right under my nose. I was to be sidetracked so I would not concentrate on his secret activities. It worked for many years, years of my spiritual, mental, and physical torture.

I should have been focusing on my children and their development rather than having to be sidetracked with this nonsense. Marc was going around the community telling people that I was delusional and that it was hard to live with me. In this book, I must tell you, readers, that I did escape intentional death at the hand of the man I trusted the most in my life: my husband. However, it was by the grace of God, my quick wit, friends, colleagues, professional people, former business associates of the so-called family, who were not afraid to help me, but there were consequences for these God-sent helpers too. One individual even lost her beloved spouse because she helped me live.

The Native American religion stands by their beliefs of generations long that say one must give up a life to save a life of one intended to die by an evil one. I did not know of this until three years later when this particular warrior told me that the night her husband lay dying on their foyer floor en route to reach his beloved wife before he took his last dying breath, she whispered to me that she heard an evil voice in her head that declared victoriously, "We can't believe that he is still alive." He died so I could live to write this book for you, to save you from what I went through in my marriage to a ruthless killer who wanted to save his millions from his wife if she ever found out his secret, the secret he tried to keep from his constituents, family, and friends that led to murder by intentional poisoning. The secret that his parents went to their grave with. He was obsessed with sex but not with his wife or other women.

Some mornings I would awaken to a strange taste in my mouth that I described as a chemical taste. On another day, I would awaken to taste salt in my mouth. Lastly, I tasted nothing but craved sugar products. Again, all of these sensations were still a mystery. Until one day, I was cleaning under our kitchen sink and found three jars of empty jewelry cleaner. Marc cleaned his Rolex watch and rings with this particular cleaner. However, one jar would last for years, unless, of course, it had another purpose. I froze in silence as I now understood what was intended with this product. After going online and reading the "poison" warning signs for this product, which is intended to clean jewelry, I suspected that he was injecting it into my right hand; it sent a fear through my mind. I now feared death. There were two kinds of this cleaner available. Marc had injected me with heavy metals. He himself was also dispensing insulin into my own vein via my right hand after he had put my own sleep medication in my diet soda before I went to bed. I was suspect of this occurring and left him a clue that I knew what he was up to. I pulled up information from the website listed on the label of the jewelry cleaner and left it on my husband's computer to let him know that I was on to him.

Now life got more dangerous for me. He would stand by our master bed and ask me questions as I passed out from whatever he put into my diet soda. He would test me by asking me various questions as I slowly passed out. He would ask, "Satin, what is your mother's middle name?" or "Do you love me, Satin?" My world would then become black. I do not recall waking up until the alarm would go off. I began to think to myself, *Why don't I wake up during the night like I used to?* It would also take a full pot of very strong coffee to get me going in the morning. Then he went to work, working on my body. I was his victim each night. I suffered from colitis of the rectum again, a nervous disorder that can take your life if it goes untreated. My gums felt as though needles had gone under my dental crowns. Then I got an infection under my crown. My crown had to be lifted and replaced at my own discretion. My dentist questioned the validity of the infections I was suffering. My head hurt from the countertop incident, but also because Marc had injected me in the back of my neck into the occipital nerve that divides the head into two. Half of my head felt like worms were crawling through it from the head injury that had occurred under the island of the kitchen bar, but the swelling of the spheroid sinuses at the top of my head was filled with fluid that was infected from my husband injecting me with his syringe into the occipital nerve. I, of course, did not know this at that time as I still lived day by day taking care of my family and my husband, always trying to figure out the mystery. My friends heard my cries and complaints. My father would say, "Satin, can't you be carefree like you used to be?" They were puzzled by these strange things I complained about. They of course never suggested that I look at my husband because they too did not want this happy, secure home to break up.

I look back at my situation today and remember saying the rosary before I fell asleep. I know that the Lord Jesus Christ was with me every night and day while I lived a life of torture by night and the facade of the most wonderful life during the day. My most envious girlfriend, Nan, reminded me of the day I had asked her how she could get up so early in the morning to teach school. You see, I was drugged every night that I slept. I was the victim of Marc's mental illnesses. He had not only one but several personalities. From my psychology background in college, I now see him being obsessive-compulsive, manic, masochistic, schizophrenic, and demonic, not to mention a psychopath. The man I had married turned into a killer. He once told me that he heard voices in his head that told him to do evil things. I had no idea what was in store for me. Was he asking for help or just leaving me a trail of clues to follow for years to come? I lived on what we used to be, not what we were, as did the family.

Little did I know at the time of my fairy-tale courtship and early marriage days with Marc that my life would be plagued with his hidden secrets. Along with his secrets were those of his family. The puzzle was complex. After Eleanor had made the statement to me that I was a very bright girl and that I would figure everything out one day, it took me twenty more years to do so. My gut feelings were always stimulated from day to day, and I spent a lot of time trying to interpret them. It was very uncomfortable for me and those close to me. I worried that my children and friends would, as I called it, feel my feelings. Sensitive people could and often did feel what I was feeling. I worried about losing friends and becoming estranged from my own children and stepchildren. I lived in beautiful surroundings but did not feel beautiful inside of myself. Instead, I could feel the secrets and deception of Marc and his evil deeds. When I would complain of this, he would again say, "Satin, count your blessings. Look what I all give you: a million-dollar home to live in, a Lincoln to drive, your own kids, and stepchildren." The list went on and on, and the big one mentioned was that I never had to work. I did not buy it, though. Never was I so plagued with negative feelings being directed to me as I experienced here.

Most of these ill-willed feelings were not being intentionally sent to me all the time, but rather, I was feeling the conflict Marc was experiencing emotionally himself about his constant conflict with his own sexual identity. After Geoff solicited Marc into friendship by sharing political interests, Marc was torn between Geoff and me. At first Marc was exuberant about his newfound friendship. He came home excited, like a new kid who just got a new bike. His statement to me was something on this order: "Satin, you and I are like Mutt and Jeff. We will be together forever, right?" Well, we had been. I said yes but wondered, *What is he up to now?* What I did not realize was that Marc was stating to me that our relationship was strong enough for him to give his extra time and friendship to a bisexual married man whom he would eventually fall in love with and force me out of our long-term marriage.

The second indication of doom came one evening after one of Marc's meetings. We had always trusted each other, but this particular evening was different. Marc did not call after the meeting to say that he would be late. We were to go out after it. Instead, I felt a cheating spouse, leaving me physically and emotionally "alone" with the kids. It was different. Matter of fact, our two kids and I drove to a local bar/club on an instinct.

There he sat outside on the patio with the members of the club. I found his car in the lot.

Our daughter was about seven years of age. She said, "Mom, I will find Dad and ask him why he did not come home to us or call." Sharnell did just that while Josh stayed in the car to calm me. She found her dad sitting at a circular table on the patio with his arms folded over his large belly to cover it up. This is what my strong little girl said: "Dad, Mother is expecting you to come home now." She stood with her hands on her chubby little hips. He adored her. Another woman at the table remarked, "Well, I guess we all can see who wears the pants in your family." Marc laughed and said that he would be home later. Sharnell stood strong and would not move until her dad walked out with her. That is how it went down. She drove home with him to make sure that her words would not go unnoticed.

During this time, I spent every Tuesday morning going to a small informal Mass with only twelve people. I prayed that I would get my husband back. I could not stop him from seeing Geoff. They were both from foreign countries, were married to women, were parents, and loved ethnic food and gay sex. I had not yet found out about the gay sex at this point, only the interest Geoff had for Marc. I begged Marc to ignore Geoff and part ways. They already knew that they were a gay match. Geoff was using Marc to get him elected to a political office. This made Marc feel important and needed. Geoff worked on Marc's ego. Geoff also brought to our home ethnic food he had prepared just for Marc. I complained to Marc that this was very abnormal, but he ignored me.

Geoff had a food stand at our local fair. It was in the summer. Marc and I attended. Geoff made a big fuss over him but ignored me completely. He gave me very little food but heaped Marc's plate full of ethnic food. Then we went to sit down at the tables and chairs provided us on this peaceful summer day, I thought, only to find Geoff totally obsessed with my husband. Geoff had left his stand and gazed right into Marc's eyes, with his mouth drooling for him. Now I knew that this was a situation to observe and question. Marc blew it off as if it was a one-way interest on Geoff's part.

Marc had always had an advantage over me since I was raised in a small town and very naive. A mockingbird could fly over my head without me noticing because I just did not believe that the bird would fly right over my head.

One morning I was showering in our master bath when I had made my request to Marc that he spend more time with me since the kids were all busy in school. He replied back saying that he was out there looking for someone to love him. I replied, "But I love you." It did not matter. I thought this was my fault because my father had died and my family had disintegrated. Social worker types are so understanding. We could dismiss anything because we know the "why" of everything. I did just that.

Marc never wanted to meet couple friends. His friends were men whom he did not share with me. I can recall four men friends whom I was introduced to by Marc at one time or another over our long marriage. He would tell me to leave them alone because they were his friends. They were lunch buddies that included way more than lunch. If Marc would change his plans and give in to my request for lunch, these men would act out verbally or physically. One man left our office and kicked Marc's car tire. The other one said so loudly on the phone that I heard him say, "But I thought today was OUR day." Yet another man was hired to put up shelves in our commercial garage. He ended up sitting in our kitchen, on our computer. He did not speak to me but looked down and never looked me in the eyes. Marc had given him personal credit cards to start a business is the story that I was told. I left my spouse with our two children for six months because he was verbally abusive and emotionally missing around this time. Emotionally missing was my most common reference to Marc's behavior and state of mind.

So my soon-to-be ex-spouse bought me a house to live in. I was in a three-bedroom apartment with our two children for six months. The youngest, Sharnell, was in kindergarten; and Josh was in second grade. I had to leave our home since I had signed a prenuptial should the occasion arise. After six months, Marc begged me to come home and that he would behave. "Behave" is a strange word to use when the person is GAY. Remember I did not know the facts at this time, however. Marc then sold the house that he had purchased for me, to the man who sat at our computer. He was married with a family too. Something went wrong with Marc's plan with this one. He sued Marc for $25,000. I was told that he had won the case. For the shrewd businessman Marc was known to be, this was not in the normal range to even discuss. It was blackmail. I can only surmise what the blackmail or money was paid to cover up. It could have been my spouse's reputation. It is not popular to be married to a woman and cheating on her with a man who is married with children also.

Along came another strange man into my home. He had a tattoo on his arm, and I had a gut feeling that he had been in prison as a juvenile. I could not find a record on him, but Marc had hired him to get rid of bats in our attic. He had found him at a homeless shelter where pedophiles were welcome. Now Marc's neighbor at the office questioned Marc why he would bring such a character around his own wife. I was not afraid of anyone from the outside but should have been. I was assuming that Marc knew that this man was gay and no threat to his wife. It ended up that this man had intentionally spilled white paint down my kitchen cupboard and drew a big bat on our kitchen floor with white paint after I fired him.

I recall another beautiful Sunday when we had gone for a drive. Marc wanted to stop at a new place that housed homeless men. I researched later that the facility housed pedophiles. This pit stop took place just prior to Marc hiring this stranger to be at home alone with his own wife and mother of his children.

Yet another man and his wife came into the picture. I think she was in on the fact that her husband was gay. Everywhere I went, they would be there it seemed, and they would ask me, "Where is Marc?" Maybe they had a sexual threesome? Why else would this lady be so interested in Marc as much as her husband? This episode went on for a year. Their son was the same age as Josh. They did not want to have anything to do with me, just Marc. It was always that way. He would isolate me from these people who would stay in our life for a year or so then disappear. It was this man who had commented to Marc that he did not wish to give up "their" day together for lunch and whatever else that included.

The last person who comes to my mind who intrigued Marc was a teacher. This man indicated to me that there was more than lunch at stake here when he kicked Marc's car tire when their planned midday rendezvous was postponed because of me. Again, I was invited to meet this man and his family at their home once. His wife was a dreary person, and he had commented to Marc that she spent a lot of time with her sister. I guess she would have to if her husband is having affairs with other men.

I cannot leave out of the gay equation yet another man. He was very handsome and intelligent. His wife was intelligent but not as pretty as him. They had done well for themselves. When my marriage was struggling, he and Marc had disappeared for a weekend together for a retreat. I believe the purpose was to show Marc that he too could live happily married and still gay. His wife was also seen in a threesome all over town. It consisted of her spouse and her mother. The leftover partner has to find emotional support of some kind to offset her spouse's affairs. In this book, I have illustrated to you that the woman's emotional support after her husband deserts her emotionally is either a child, mother, sister, or another boyfriend. If it should be another woman other than family, chances are that they would be lesbians.

The leftover woman feels less than second best. She is not the love of his life. He may go so far as to put on a special anniversary recognition publicly for the locals to see, hoping to remove any question whether this is a heterosexual relationship between the woman and the man who married at one time and produced children. He may display pictures of the couple in their earlier and happier years together, before acting on his gay side. One common photo would be of the happy couple who are expecting their first baby. The gay man does not always show his true sexual identity until he is in his late fifties. It is now that he is financially secure. The family is raised. The family unit is not questioned by each other or the public. There are high risks to face should the wife leave the marriage at this point. The children would have to believe her side of things, but the children will be upset with whoever pulls out of the family unit. Believe me, I know how it works.

Your "self" is what it is all about. Cheating on a spouse is abuse in itself. Threatening anyone into secrecy or trying to make your partner look mentally unstable to cover up the side of yourself you are hiding is not feasible. Trying to maintain a powerful position in the community rests mostly on "What kind of family man is he?"

You can fool someone for a while, but in reality, it is a short while. People find the truth. They begin to talk and share stories of what they have seen or heard throughout the community. You cannot hide yourself from yourself. It all comes to the surface. I like to compare it to oil on top of water. I was the oil. He was the water. I floated. He was the dirty water trying to clean itself, still. He cannot purify the vast ocean of water he has dirtied with his lies, physical and mental abuse, coercion of his children, stealing, and cheating. Now his dreams keep him restless. His health keeps him worried. He is fearful to face eternity, not knowing where it will be or whom it will be with, if anyone.

I pity the man who tried to take my life by intending to give me poison on a vacation of doom. I pity the man I once loved, who broke promises. I am not understanding of his situation as I once was. God help us for being so trusting and naive.

CHAPTER 30

Marc Refuses to Have Sex with Me

TIME WENT ON, and Marc became involved in local politics. I thought it was a good outlet for him at first. He was gone only on Wednesday nights, and I was happy with that. Next, he ran for another office and was elected to serve four years. His meetings increased to three nights per week. His ego was so depleted from being an overweight boy that he had to prove something to himself and others. His popularity increased, and he was good in the political arena. His ideas and plans were beneficial to the community.

I supported him, but we were suffering at home. Everyone came before me or the children. After my father died, our son was only ten years of age, and Sharnell was only seven. Marc announced to me that he had helped me raise his two eldest children but that he was walking out on us, the remaining family, simply to have a life of his own. He didn't want a divorce but wanted to leave us. The divorce was out of the question because of money. He wanted to shed the family and live a life of his own. His office became his home. The huge house became mine with the two remaining children of ours.

I went to my part-time job feeling empty, feeling single but married. I called it "loved but alone." My job became my salvation. By now I was working as a beautician in an assisted-living facility. It was there I had emotional support, and my clients became my family. This position lasted for three full years.

By this time, my own mother was losing her memory, and my husband had left me. I kept thinking that he had replaced us for his political career, but the truth was that he came home one normal day, I thought, saying, "Satin, I am attracted to Geoff, and I think he is cute." I was in shock and responded, "Excuse me?" For days he talked about his newfound friend, Geoff. Geoff owned a local cafe and was a "wannabe" politician. They both shared ethnic similarities. Their friendship was like two male peas in a pod. Every day he talked about Geoff. He ate breakfast and lunch at his cafe every weekday. Marc got Geoff appointed to a political office. Geoff hired our daughter, Sharnell, to work at the cafe. I had told Marc to stay away from this man. He promised that he would but did not and lied to me.

My woman employer called me into her office and told me about a gay friend of hers. She told me that she believed my husband was gay too. I could not accept this truth. I did not cry but went on alone, just trying to survive. It was my job to keep the family together, I thought. I went on alone for the next three years. My husband entertained our governor-elect at our home with many guests. Geoff approached me in the kitchen of our stately home at the party and said, "Satin, why don't you take that noose off your husband's neck?" I had never met Geoff and did not know that he even existed prior to six months earlier. He was the man whom I had felt in Marc and our relationship earlier. It was he who had taken my place as Marc's lover and best friend. I was still in denial. Marc would not have sex with me and would sit on our bed with his arms around his legs, protecting his penis from my touch. I would sit on a chair next to our bed and try to convince him to have sex with me. He would respond with "I am not going to do that." I would try to negotiate with him. At one point, around Easter, I suggested that we have sex; and he reluctantly agreed to. As he lay on our bed comforter with me on top, he had a large erection but started to rub his forehead in confusion and was not emotionally there. He responded with this strange statement: "I don't know who I even am anymore." I knew at that moment that he was in fact gay. He refused to have sex with his wife and didn't know what gender he really was. I was crushed. I immediately called my friends who had been married for years. I went there after Marc left the house, and together we looked for a psychologist in the Yellow Pages of the local phone book. I knew that I would be divorced and that I would be misplaced and no longer have a home or security. My world fell apart, but I kept this a secret from the little kids. I called my stepson and his natural mother and told them about what Marc was saying and how he had changed. Jake could not relate, but his mother listened carefully. None of us had known him in this state. I was alone with this. Marc's mind would switch from female to male and back within a split second.

Geoff would come to our house with food trays and gifts for Marc. The gifts were not for me or the family. Marc would not let me cook in the kitchen. The kitchen of our 6,200-square-foot house was always considered my domain for preparing special family dishes, making gourmet dinners for family and friends, but now was reclaimed by Marc. Only he could cook in my space. Also, sex with me was taboo. I was replaced by Geoff. My best attribute in my marriage was the fact that I cooked well and our sex life was great. I took Marc to a licensed nurse practitioner in a mental health center, out of town of course. I was told that he could be gay and that he had split-personality disorder plus OCD: obsessive-compulsive disorder. He was directed to take a drug called Luvox, which would put his personality together into one. He lasted on the drug for two weeks, and he was my husband again until Geoff came into his office and had asked Marc where he had been for the past couple of weeks. Then Geoff asked Marc if he had cleared their relationship with me since he had done so with his wife. Marc would dream and talk about Geoff in his sleep. His conversation with himself in his sleep related in verbiage to his sexual relation with Geoff. One night I awoke to Marc repeating over and over, "Ooh, ah, does it feel as good for you as it does for me?'" I jabbed him in the arm. I said, "Marc, what are you doing?" He replied, "Oh, I must be getting a massage." My psychiatrist suggested that Marc was reliving a sexual encounter that he had already had with Geoff. He spoke about Geoff constantly. He raced out of the house in the wee hours of the morning without breakfast each and every day, including Saturdays. He had always had breakfast at a fast-food chain each morning. I knew where this was and had asked an employee friend of mine to watch who he had for company there. She described his bisexual male friend who had come to our home one fall evening for a drive in another friend's car. I began to find out just who associated with whom. They were all gay men living with wives. I never knew where he was going. One morning, I mumbled in my sleep, "I sure am glad that I am not you." He replied, "Be glad that you do not walk in my shoes, Satin."

The puzzle was not complete. Marc still loved me too. He would come home and lie on the couch with his legs crossed like a woman. He would sit at his desk and curl his hair with his forefinger. His mind was always distant and on something else. If I stopped at his office, he would be taking a nap in the afternoon. When he would get home in the early afternoon sometimes, he would have already washed out his white underwear, saying that he had had diarrhea. Really, he wanted to get rid of any sexual evidence of adultery: another man's sperm on his own underwear. In later months, he would smell like feces, and he would reply that he could not help it that he had a "leaky asshole."

He had developed a large tumor under his scrotum that had to be lanced and drained by a doctor in our local hospital's emergency room. The doctor walked by me in the hall, shaking his head in disgust as he looked at me sympathetically. Gay men often develop a tumor as such from the bacteria of sperm not being able to drain out of the rectum completely.

I was tested for AIDS every six months and lived in fear of getting the dreaded disease. When I approached the clinic's lab, the technicians would look at me and quietly chuckle behind the counter. I complained to the staff president, and their jobs were all threatened because of the HIPAA laws. I was no longer a popular person but now shunned in the community. I looked for support from friends and also a male friend who would stand by me for up to a year after I left the illness. My doctor suggested that I get tested at our local blood donation center. He said that if I should ever get a disease of this nature, my health insurance could be discontinued.

CHAPTER 31

The Morning Shower Terror

ABOUT THE TIME I was asking Marc to spend some quality time with me when I had suggested that he stay away from the man he called Geoff. One weekday morning, I had asked him to pick us up breakfast and bring it home. He agreed reluctantly and had called Geoff to tell him of his delay in meeting him! Well, I went to take my morning shower and heard Marc enter our master bath when he threw a bag from a fast food into the sink near the shower. He said, "Well, I gotta go!" so I, through the shower door, bargained with him by saying, "Come on, Marc, let's spend some time together." To my surprise, he became very angry and grabbed his hair on his head, pulling it so hard that I thought he would for sure be bald! He then screamed loudly, "I have to get rid of you!" as he ground his teeth together. He repeated this over and over! I began to shake with fear as sudden terror went through my naked body! I know he thought about grabbing a kitchen butcher knife as he remained in the kitchen for a minute! I held my breath in total silence as I thought to myself that he could actually come back into the bathroom and "bleed me out!" acting as unstable as he had recently become! This was the man who ran our city council! The police would never believe me should I call! He knew that, and should he have killed me, he would have blamed it on an intruder!

This was about the time in our relationship when I caught Marc petting his dog, named Mullet, over and over repeating, a man's name in error. When I had confronted him on this, he got up from his desk chair in our kitchen and chased me around the island until I grabbed my purse, without a coat, and ran to my car, locked it, and tore out of the driveway on a Saturday morning! Later I returned to ignore him after he had taken our daughter Sharnell out shopping. He told her I was having a delusion!

Again, I got no help from the police. If I called, they would come and tell me that if I felt unsafe, I should move out! With no place to go, I lived my life alone and kept my distance from Marc and Geoff. Of course the day came when I had been so poisoned that I ended up in the emergency room in a small town forty miles from home! It was that day I had to face my fear of leaving my house and children to save my own life from what would come next!

CHAPTER 32

New Laws for Me in the House

MARC WOULD TRY to keep me in the public eye with him when he was at political functions, but Geoff would be angry when he saw me with my husband of almost twenty-five years and would give me nasty looks. Marc still wanted both of us, but Geoff did not want a threesome. As I continued my personal investigation of my life and the people involved in the secret, my life was threatened.

One particular weekday afternoon, I found my husband sitting at the end of our large kitchen table waiting until I got home. He told me that I had become a problem to him and that I would have to seek a full-time job to support myself and that he would only pay for the house bills, not mine. He would buy me only a cheap little car to get me by instead of an expensive vehicle as he had done in the past. There would be no more vacations together as he would take his alone. He had been doing that most of our married life as it was, leaving me as a dogsitter and babysitter. He warned me to shut my mouth if I knew what was good for me. He said his office was to be his home except to sleep and that the house would be my space with our young teenage children who were left to raise.

He said that he had warned me before, but word had gotten back to him that I was not content with our present situation. He told me that I was the "only" woman in his life for him, but if I did leave him, there would be a replacement. His telling me to count my blessings when I complained was now over. He had been advised what to do with me and how to do whatever was planned for my fate by his gay colleagues. My fear heightened. Now I was being followed by a little old man in a burgundy van. This little man would be seen when I went out for lunch; and he would walk into the restaurant, sit in a booth near mine, and take notes. He would remain there until I would leave. So I would not leave. Then the unthinkable happened. I was leaving my job as a beautician with an elderly resident. We were headed out of town about twenty minutes away to a large truck stop with an adjacent gift shop. I was in total fear that day; my body shook inside. As we walked into the front door of the large complex, we witnessed two men in top hats and trench coats storm into the back door that was directly in front of us about sixty feet away. I was to be kidnapped. By my taking Evelyn with me that day saved me from kidnapping. Marc had gotten up that last Sunday morning early, and I found him sitting in our large great room, cupping his hands with his face buried into them. He was sobbing uncontrollably and repeating loudly to himself that he had to get rid of me. I was confused and naive. What he was really saying was that he had planned my demise. Victims live in denial. That is the "why" of how women die at the hand of their own spouse. It is because they do not believe that the person they loved and married would ever really harm them. Statistics show differently, however.

We have been taught by traditional religion to trust, love, cherish, and embellish God's grace and protection if we truly are Christians. This false teaching has been responsible for many domestic murders. It was my experience that people want to believe the best and shut their eyes to the truth in hope that somehow if they close their mind and ears to open, visual signs of abuse and abnormalities, they would not exist. I blame this on traditional false beliefs taught to us in churches, that what is seen is. It is NOT. People change. People become swayed and mentally ill. People torture and kill. People plot and hide their abuse then hide the evidence of their abuse or victims.

You may ask yourself, "How can she be such a heretic? How can she be so unsaved?" My girlfriend had me interviewed with an FBI agent when I was so scared in my marriage. He told me to get in touch with him when I felt my life was in danger. However, when I needed him, he had retired.

Geoff cornered me on our city street one day. He looked at me eyeball to eyeball and said, "You better shut your mouth or I will get someone to silence you for good." I was terrified. I immediately walked over to the local police department and reported the threat. I was taken to a back room that was the size of one of our bathrooms in our big house. There I was asked to sit across from an officer. Another unidentified woman officer stood behind this particular officer. Lastly, we were joined by a sergeant who stood in the corner of this small room. I made a formal complaint that I was threatened with my life by Geoff. Geoff was now a local politician. Marc was also. The officer behind the desk laughed at me and said that Geoff was simply joking. This was not considered a threat. Then we looked up the word "threat" on the computer. Again, I was told that this was not considered a threat even though Geoff had parked behind me, blocking my way out of a city parking lot adjacent to his cafe prior to this incident several months earlier. At that time, I had questioned my husband why he didn't confront his buddy, Geoff, for this attack on his wife. I got no response from him either. Political people have a generic way of doing nothing about anything that puts them in between two individuals whom they have split interests. To my surprise, the officer behind the desk took his thumbs and stuck them in his ears, wagging his fingers and sticking his tongue out at me, reciting this mantra: "Hey, Satin, look at this." Then he recited, "Gnaw, gnaw, gnaw, gnaw, gnaw, gnaw," with high and low notes. To my amazement, I was witnessing police abuse. I was being made fun of with witnesses of the department laughing and tantalizing me, a concerned citizen of the community who had just been threatened with my life at stake. I was so afraid that I hurried to my lawyer's office to repeat to him what had indeed happened to me. He guessed it before I had even opened my mouth. He replied that he had heard of this before. My reality of a kind, caring police officer holding a lost child's hand now fled from my confused and weary mind.

After that incident, police officers watched my car everywhere I went within the city. I was even followed by the police for no apparent reason. Now I knew that they could be ordered to pick me up for simply anything that I did not commit as a normal citizen. I pictured myself in jail for a setup. I became even more terrified than what I had lived in my home before I had left my evil husband. Now I could see a setup by these evil department heads on our police force in a large city.

Reality set in even more when my girlfriend had set me up on a date with a man who had dated a woman from our local area. I had heard of a police brutality story he had relayed to me from her. She was getting a divorce from a man of substantial wealth who had hired dirty cops to go to their home and scare her into settling financially with a very low settlement. Police had knocked on her door, she let them in, and they forced her to the floor and then proceeded to step on her neck. They had her in a hold by stepping on her neck for no reason other than money paid by her soon-to-be ex-husband. This guy dated me for three months but warned me to keep my apartment door locked and not to open it for a cop. If one did come to the door, he instructed me to remain silent within my home but then call 911 for another police officer to witness the scene by remaining safe inside my home. I knew he was indeed telling the truth, and I heeded it by calling our mayor, who was aware of my present situation because he was a buddy to my husband. He refused the phone call; and I knew Sara, who was the mayor's secretary, directed me to call the city attorney's office. I unloaded my story and my own concerns to seek safety in a corruptly run city where the sheep all felt safe.

Spreading my story to more people made me feel safer because more people would know what I was experiencing if I should just simply disappear out of the blue. So not only did I live in fear before I left my house, but after leaving him and living alone presented another set of problems. My divorce was planned to run for two years to bleed me of my funds, but the excuse was that there were not enough judges to go around on the circuit. The woman I really wanted to take my case charged $800 per hour and was known for representing divorces of the famous baseball players of our state. She was the one gal who could have set up residence in this community, but she opted out by telling me that I needed to secure a seasoned attorney in our fine city and that I simply could not afford her. Later, I realized that the money I had lost to corruption here would have been obtained in righteousness and I would have come out better in the long run.

My first lawyer enabled me to get an apartment in the building that my husband owned. Marc had just put our daughter in it after high school and made her his apartment manager. Then he caused strife between mother and daughter by having her "kicked out" of it only to go back to our big house. Here she had moved in and decorated it as an independent young lady that she was only to be humiliated to find out that her mother needed it in order to stay off the streets. Married, our assets were approximately four million dollars; but if Mom left Dad, she would be on the streets. My daughter hated me at that time; Marc kept telling her that I was crazy and delusional. He wanted her on his side. He played her against me. She hated me and told me to leave her apartment when I had nowhere else to go before my first divorce hearing. She left her apartment in rage by tearing pictures off the walls; disconnecting her TV; and taking all of the towels, soap, shower curtain, and stereo with her as she drove off in her dad's new truck with her girlfriend, Carla. Marc was happy that he had turned our daughter against me. It was 2:00 a.m. when I found myself stripped of a daughter, sitting alone in an apartment that was awarded to me to live in during my divorce. My daughter laughed with her girlfriend as they drove off in Marc's new red truck. I sat on the couch that was too big for Sharnell to take with her and sobbed. Finally, I called my Jewish friend, Rose, to be consoled. The next day, she called to tell me not to call that late ever again because her husband could not get back to sleep. There are "friends," and then there are true friends.

CHAPTER 33

How I Left My Husband

I MOVED INTO ROBERTA'S house in our neighborhood only four nights before I was to board a plane to Puerto Vallarta with my husband who had murder on his mind. It was Friday, April 13. Today as I write this book for you it is April 17.

Each and every day that I celebrate my life, I remember Friday, April 13. This is the day that my life was spared from the evilness that had surrounded me for years as the wife of a rich politician. It was today that I would wake up to find a new life of struggle yet knowledge before me. I would be liberated in America after being held captive by my own husband's torture by night and brainwashing during the day. Too afraid to move out of his sight, unable to find even an apartment owner who would rent to me with $150,000 of my own money without a job.

I awoke again with a sense of struggle as to what day I would escape this encampment that I had become accustomed to living in. My friends had deserted me, saying they did not want to see me die at the hands of my husband.

I had a deadline to work around this time. We had a trip planned out of the country. I was afraid always. When I would come out of the grocery store, I would fear that Marc would set me up with a dead body in the trunk of my vehicle only for the carryout boy to find when he put my groceries in it. Thinking like this does not just happen.

Since I was a third-generation psychic, I was sensing what others questioned about my spouse. Was he a cold-blooded killer? Or had he singled out his wife to kill to save his money from her knowing it would be a costly divorce? No matter what, living conditions for Mrs. Silverstein were not healthy, the doctor had told her.

On Friday, April 13, the ER doctor said, "You have to leave your husband today, Mrs. Silverstein, or I believe that you will become a mere statistic in the world of murdered wives. You must leave him today or he will kill you, I am afraid. The way you speak of him. The fear in your voice. The strange things he is saying to you. Your swollen tongue and throat, elevated blood pressure so high that we fear you having a stroke before our very eyes indicates intended foul play here. You spoke of screaming at the top of your lungs in your upstairs bedroom, but neither your children nor your husband coming to your aid is a sure indication of a torture that you are yet to suffer. You now have had an internal warning from Mr. Silverstein. We want to call the sheriff in our small city here and put you in a safe house until arrangements can be made for you to securely leave your home with support. The catch, however, is we would have to make you a vulnerable adult to carry this plan out. We must protect ourselves from any lawsuit Mr. Silverstein may impose on our hospital here. Are you willing to do this?" After a fearful deliberation of the situation, I found myself saying "no."

"I will make arrangements for myself to leave him when he is at the meeting on Monday night," I said. This would be the hardest thing I had ever done in my life. I could not back out as Monday night was to be my escape night or else I would face death on my trip to Mexico the next day. My heart was racing at the thought. Now, I could and would only depend on myself. The self is very important. I know that I have the strongest self, like a true warrior. I am a warrior for myself. My own psychiatrist was threatened with Marc calling him, threatening to sue the clinic if he helped me. He was to set up my hometown hospital lab to do a toxicology report should Marc poison me within the next month. I had called the doctor's office, which was one hour away, to talk to him. I told his nurse that it was an emergency. She said that he refused to talk to me. He, at the last minute, had been threatened his position at the clinic if he should help me. I was happy that I could finally depend on myself. I do not let myself down very often. This book is intended to show the readers what it means to have fear turned into power, strength, honor, integrity, righteousness, dignity, and, lastly but the most important, faith in the Creator who guided my every minute of this long journey to freedom from the killer, my husband. There he was baffled at the hand of God holding mine

FAIRY TALE TO MURDER

until I crossed a new path of life not yet intended to take the spiritual path to the white light. I am now a free woman but still haunted with the memories that this book brings to my mind. I now still feel fear from this man and what he has the capacity to do. It is real fear. I know evil and what a sick mind can produce. I will never be the same girl who was carefree going to high school. I will look over my shoulder for the rest of my life, but my readers must know the truth of survival and how a *Romeo and Juliet* story turned out to be *Silence of the Lamb*.

I called dear friends, loaded two cars full to the top with black garbage bags that contained my belongings, and went to find refuge at my friend's home only one block from my house. There I remained for three months. My children were being brainwashed each day by their father that I was having an affair. My children were embarrassed that their home had broken up, and Marc blamed the whole thing on me and his made-up sickness story. He actually called my friends and his family saying that I was having a delusion and that no one knew where I was. He commented that the family was very worried on my whereabouts. Each and every day he would drive by my car, stop, open it up, and put an earring he had taken from my jewelry box in the past year or so and put it on the sun visor of the driver's side. I had to get my car locks changed. My apartment lock had to have a special lock. I always traveled with another person.

The men I dated carried a pistol with them. I took gun training and received a permit to carry a license. Life changed for me. I am not afraid to defend myself any longer. I will shoot to kill as instructed if anyone should break into my home. My daughter became a police officer. She has a lot to learn about her dad. I hope she reads this book. In her career, she too will see corruption, but she won't talk to me about it. She is a smart girl. I have faith that at the end of her career, she will know what I have learned about this community and others. I do not want her to be a sheep but rather a sheepdog, one who protects the sheep. "Do you believe there are wolves out there who will feed on the flock without mercy? You better believe it. There are evil men in this world, and they are capable of evil deeds. The moment you forget that or pretend it is not so, you become a sheep. There is no safety in denial" (*On Sheep, Wolves, and Sheepdogs,* Dave Grossman). Now I do not have to wake up with bruises and pain in my chest any longer from the abuse my husband inflicted on me while he had put me in a deep sleep from sleeping pills, nor do I have to suffer the whole day or several days with the pain he inflicted on me in his evil mental illness state. I remember my psychiatrist from my hometown asking me to take off my clothes to examine my body after I was divorced. He had seen the bruises before and now said, "Case closed: no marks or bruises." He had warned me after seeing my porcelain doll's broken face which Marc had inflicted on her, that my spouse was intending to kill me since brainwashing me that I was delusional and crazy did not work. Also, the local Battered Women's Shelter had told me the same thing after seeing the doll. Marc had broken the doll's neck, poked a screwdriver through her forehead, and took a pear-shaped piece out of her right cheek. Keep in mind the porcelain piece was missing from the crime scene as well as the piece of terry cloth that had been cut out of my bathrobe. I first saw the results of Marc's savage attack on this doll after taking my morning shower. It had happened similar to the incident when he had cut a hole out of the right breast area of my yellow terry cloth bathrobe. I was again scared and horrified. I had found the screwdriver that had pierced the doll's forehead in our garage on top of the metal locker that contained sporting equipment from our kids. The screwdriver was a Phillips. Both sources, the psychiatrist and the Battered Women's Shelter advocate, had said exactly the same thing: Marc really wanted to do this to me but rather did it to objects at this time.

During the last part of my marriage, I felt so unsafe at night while I slept that I made my own bedroom upstairs right above the master bedroom. I had gone as far as to hire a locksmith to install a deadbolt lock on my upstairs bedroom door. The first night that I locked it and was feeling a bit safer shocked me even more. I woke up to find that Marc had come upstairs during the night with a tool kit and had removed the complete doorknob. There I was sleeping unprotected from my husband again after spending $100 to have this deadbolt lock installed the day before. So the next night I put a heavy bedroom rocking chair in front of the door because my girlfriend told me that she suspected that Marc was doing all of these sick things to me. I thought if he barged into the room, I would at least awaken. That is exactly what happened. I awoke to the heavy rocking chair toppling over on the carpet and Marc storming into the room. He came in with full body force along the left side of my queen-size bed. He acted as though he was sleepwalking. I said, "Marc, what are you doing?" He responded strangely, saying, "Nobody is going to keep me from my fucking wife." I responded with "Everything is okay here. You can go back to bed now. I love you." He left and went out of the room. Every night, I slept with my hands crossed over my heart. This protected me from spiritual attack, I thought, as I slumbered. It did not protect me from physical attack of any nature. Marc kept telling me that I was being attacked by demons from the medicine men whom I went to for advice about this weird situation. He wanted me to keep my mind off him. He allowed me much freedom with my time and did not keep tabs on my whereabouts during the day until just before I left. Then he had hired a man to follow me as I went out for lunch. I had caught this man several times.

As I have mentioned before, he was very understanding of my responsibility I felt I had for my ailing mother who suffered from Alzheimer's disease after my father had passed away from bladder cancer, which had spread rapidly to his lymph nodes. He died from lung cancer within only three weeks of us finding out that he was ill. I would weekly go to see my mother or bring her to our home. He always treated her with respect and dignity while he tortured her daughter during the night. I would go to sleep thinking that God would spare me from whatever this was if I prayed to Him. I fell asleep often praying the rosary. I had a strong faith that was actually instilled by my mother who herself had been abused and had internally abused me. My parents liked Marc, and so did most of our friends, but my father never trusted him and taught my brother not to discuss any of our family business with him. We liked to entertain and had friends around the house. People liked to come for fine food and good conversation on special occasions or Sundays. We provided this for them and supplied all of the food. Our guests were treated like royalty. They did not return the favor, either because they felt inferior or because they thought we had the money to spend, so why should they? Marc never wanted to socialize with people who had more money or prestige than us. So I had created my own family of friends. These same friends emotionally supported me for the years it took me to figure out my at-home living situation. Marc had always had his parents to himself while we were married. If anything, I was on the outside with our kids. They were not. Matter of fact, his parents would visit him at the office before they would come to our home. I got blamed for locking my house door during the day to be safe. They said that I was trying to keep them out of our home when they would visit from out of state. I was to be following an open-door policy.

I would prepare special meals when they were in town. But my mother-in-law would either start an argument or sneak off to another room to hide some witchcraft object she came in with from her purse. Finally, after her last episode of doing this, Marc agreed with me that his own mother could not come into our home, and she remained an outlaw for ten years. This enabled him to take two vacations alone to their residence since his mother could not get along with me. So by being "bad," she was rewarded with her son alone for a full week's worth. In return for the favor of me allowing my husband to see her this way, I would receive a lovely gift of fine clothing from her favorite store, which I liked as well. It was a win-win situation for us both. I got clothes and did not have to put up with her or the fear she brought with her. She got her son. Andes, Marc's dad, died a year after I escaped Marc and his abuse. Eleanor herself lived another year past that. Marc called me and told me not to attend his dad's funeral. However, when I regained access of our big house, I found a stack of sympathy cards he had saved for me to view that he had received from his dad's funeral. Besides the cards, which had my friends' names on some of them, I found a pile of cleaning rags, a mop, a pail, and a Dyson vacuum cleaner in the utility room. My shiny black grand piano remained in the formal living room next to the sixteen-foot Norway pine tree that I had nurtured every week for twenty-five years. This tree had luscious foliage and had been moved and repotted from the sunroom to the large formal living room that had a seventeen-foot ceiling, allowing more than adequate growth. This tree had served as the children's Christmas tree for them to decorate each year until it had outgrown that room and had advanced into the formal living room. Sad to say, at the sale of this prestigious home, there was not a church or place to donate it to except for the Boy Scout office that the realtor who had found me a new home came up with. It was unwrapped before moving, and its luscious foliage had been torn and tattered. It too had struggled to survive.

Our younger children suffered the most. The eldest were married with their own homes and families. All in all, we all suffered, but I was to blame. I had broken up the home, the house everyone shared so many fond memories of.

Marc also raped from me the proceeds I was to obtain from the sale of this huge home. A buyer appeared to Marc while we were separated and had offered him a very good price for the house. I was called to sign papers to sell the home from Marc's realtor. At the last minute, when I was responding to her request for me to sign papers to sell the home, her office staff could not find her. I thought this was strange. Finally, I received a call from the real estate office to wait until Monday. By Monday, the buyers had backed out of the deal with the excuse, I was told, that their young children were not sleeping well and the parents did not feel that they could proceed with the sale or take on any remodeling project at this time. I found this to be a fishy excuse, and indeed it was. Marc and his long-term lady friend realtor had discussed my obtaining the home as a divorce settlement. This would rape me of the "just due" proceeds by waiting until the market dropped, and the buyers could purchase it at almost half the asking price, which would have been $500,000, instead of $1 million. My lawyer was in on a cut as well, to my disbelief. He had made an "under the table" deal with Marc that would include but not be exclusive to refusing to insist on us getting an appraisal of this home that would be of course my settlement. In essence, a deal had been made with Marc and the potential buyer to wait until I took the house as a settlement. I would be forced to sell it immediately to survive. These buyers could then grab it at a low price, and Marc would get top dollar for the two adjacent acres that bordered our home. That is just what the scheme was. It worked. I had no idea that the same people were told to wait for two more years to obtain the house cheaply. The housing market had dropped during the two-year divorce. I was drawing money from my own savings account to live for the two-year separation. Marc paid maintenance monies to me at this time but purposely kept a mortgage on our home that amounted to the maintenance money he spent plus income taxes for a two-year period that he purposely took out an extension for, making me pay for half of them since he had carefully planned to quit work and "float" in order to show fewer assets just prior to my filing for a divorce. The little meeting with my lawyer occurred about five months before we would have been appointed a jury in a court appearance. Even though the physical, mental, and emotional abuse was evident, my lawyer would not take the case unless I agreed not to go after Marc criminally. Very few lawyers would take the case as he was a well-known figure in the community and on the city council.

One day, my lawyer, Jeff, told me that he was meeting Marc's lawyer in order to end my two-year divorce. He told me that I would be called to come into his office on the day that the four of us would meet. I was there in his office one early weekday morning. Jeff was at his desk; Marc's attorney was in the conference room of my lawyer's office quarters. Marc opened Jeff's door and motioned him to come out into the hall. He did it quite forcefully by extending his arm from his elbow through the open door frame and ordering Jeff to join him. Jeff stood up behind his desk, leaning on it with his arms extended, repeating, "I am not going into a room with you." Later I realized that this was all a front. Today was not the planning phase of the divorce. That had already been done. Today was the "Marc pays off my lawyer and his lawyer" day. The planning had all changed months prior to this time. Jeff, my own lawyer, refused to allow us to get an appraisal of my lovely home. His excuse was that Marc would then want to appraise all of his properties. So what he should have been only concerned about was what my appraisal would be. Marc had called me into his office months earlier, saying that I would get 1.2 million and had asked me what properties I wanted. I told him the house and a rental property he had owned. He agreed. I did not expect my lawyer to "sell me down the river." He too was a good actor. When Jeff stood up at his desk, he did exactly what he had told Marc he would not do. That was that he was not going to join Marc in a room with Marc's lawyer. Then he did the unthinkable. Jeff ordered me to stay sitting in his office corner and not to enter the negotiating room with my husband, his lawyer, and himself. My response was "If you are going in there, I am too." He again ordered me to remain seated in my chair in his office. It was there, at that very moment, Jeff received payment for not appraising the homestead so I would lose half a million.

The next day, I ended up in our local hospital emergency room. I was treated for shock. My body knew the truth, but my mind had not quite figured out the actions of Jeff, my lawyer. Jeff responded in a stunned manner, when I said, "Did Marc bribe you?" He came back with "Well, if you do not trust me, Satin, I will have to withdraw from this case immediately." Keep in mind that the case was almost over, and I had made an agreement to pay this man $60,000 and had already paid him a $10,000 retainer. If we did not settle out of court at this time, our court hearing was already scheduled for the next week. There would be absolutely no time to obtain another attorney or afford to get one. The judge, as well as the jury, was already set. At our first hearing, a man walked from the back of our courtroom, proceeded to the judge's chamber, and nodded his head in agreement with my husband as Marc nodded back. That meant that this case was already set from the very beginning. Marc had set an amount to pay off the judge who presided over our divorce case, should it go from mediation to a trial with him presiding.

I had told Jeff about this nod of heads, and he got very nervous. I was sure I would not get my just amount either way. I told Jeff that I did not agree on our proposed settlement. His response was that he could not do any better and that I either take this or sit up at our remote lake house with maintenance monies from my ex-husband. He then said, "Don't expect him to pay it either, Satin."

CHAPTER 34

Terrified in the Night

RECENTLY I HAD the unexpected pleasure of meeting my adult son and his friend Mateo. We had a lovely visit, and his friend had spent many hours in our home while the boys went to school together. As we were catching up on the news, my son Josh pulled his cell phone out of his pocket to show me a photo of his girlfriend's friend who held a young child on her hip and another child's hand in her left hand. At first glimpse, she looked very similar to me when I was in my thirties. Josh commented, "Doesn't she look just like you did when you were raising Sharnell and I?"

"Yes," I replied, "she really does." He commented that he kept the photo of the strangers on his phone to think of himself, his younger sister, and me as a close family unit. Josh was remembering the close tie I had with both of my little ones during the happiest times of our lives. Now, we are in different locations, and my relationship with both children is strained because of their new lives, jobs, locations, and my divorce with their father. Their father polarized his two eldest children to his side of the family after our divorce while he was dating a new woman, even though he told me that he was gay. My "blood children" remained close to me after the anger and sadness moved past them.

After five years or so, Marc worked on resuming a relationship once again with his two youngest children. So he closed in on his two eldest children from his first wife then went to retrieve the youngest of the four children, my only blood children. This was something I did not expect to have happened. It was more painful than I would ever know. He would lie to them, telling them that I had suffered from delusions. They can see through him, but our son chose to remain with his two eldest siblings while our daughter had a bad experience with her oldest sister at her dad's home. She saw through her father's side of the family politics after being blamed for her baby niece falling out of a high chair. It was more than painful not to hear my son's pleasant voice calling once in a while, saying, "Hi, Mom." His girlfriend called him a "mama's baby" until he stopped calling. First he would call on his way home from work. Then that stopped completely. He quit answering my calls or texts. Insecure and jealous women will control their men by belittling them or calling them names.

I am thankful I had the pleasure of raising a family of four. Each child brought to the table different attributes with completely different personalities, but they still shared similarities! Liana was tall and slim; very intellectual she turned out to be. She was a "feeling" person. Our Josh was also a "feeling" person, also slim in stature. They had this in common. I mean that they received "love" by feeling the emotion. Jake and Sharnell were both, as my mother would call it, "fleshy." They were not fat but a bit overweight. They were "hearing" people. They received "love" by experiencing positive words. Thus, they were less sensitive. In a home where negative feelings floated freely from outside influences, the more sensitive children suffered more. My mother-in-law, Eleanor, took sides with Sue against us in raising Liana. Both Eleanor and Sue shared the evil support of Satanist groups from different locations. My husband, Marc, also shared a Satanist group connection by way of his mother and his bookkeeper, Sandy, and later, himself. One could never get rid of the evil feelings that spread through one family member to the next. Satanists send their ritualistic evil energy obtained in animal and human sacrifices to an innocent party. When one is near this person, the "icky" feeling passes into the intended victim. It is complicated to write about unless I address much more about how the occult works. The occult can attack a victim physically, mentally, emotionally, and/or psychically. I, over the years, was attacked in all of these areas but stayed to raise our children. I did not know that I was being attacked by Marc physically, however.

CHAPTER 35

While Writing This Book,
I Soul Traveled in My Sleep to Intervene For . . .

D URING MY SLEEP, I soul traveled unexpectedly to a family in serious trouble. I could feel the very dark, negative energy there. A man in his early thirties with strawberry blond hair, which was brushed back and shoulder length, was threatening his wife. He was ordering her to leave their marriage, the house, and their two children, who I saw huddled together in a lounge chair. It looked like a five-year-old boy and his three-year-old sister. They were scared, and I was afraid for the wife. She was cornered in the room by this very sick husband who was telling me and another man who also soul traveled to the scene that he lusted for other women and wanted to be single. He was trying to scare this mother of his children into the street and to leave her children. She could not get away from him. When she turned her body to the right, he was there. If she moved to the left, he was there in her face, threatening her and pushing his weight around over a woman half of his size who was trying to please him. She did not yet know the escape plan that I would teach her. I relived the terror my spouse imposed on me, the feeling state, and the thought he had in his head to kill her. I intervened spiritually and prayed for a big angel to spread his wings around the chair with the two little ones in it. Then

I found myself slipping into this angry man's face, while the wife made it out of the house. What she did not realize, as I didn't either, was just how volatile each moment in the presence of this insane man could potentially be. Her life could have been "snuffed out" by this threatening, abusive, mentally unstable man just as my life could have been taken by a mentally ill psychopath, leaving my two young children motherless! All day I prayed for her. I wondered who she was and how my spiritual intervention had sustained her during those critical minutes of attack from her husband. "Oh, dear one, hear my thought to you. Take the children and leave when he is gone, before he takes your life." This is the first time I have interceded by soul travel on behalf of another human being. When we are "spiritual warriors," God directs us to soul travel to those in desperate need. We have learned from our situation and are then used to intervene and help others who are actually experiencing crisis at that very minute. As God ordered other Christians to pray for us during our crisis, possibly waking them up in the middle of the night to intervene in prayer for us, we too are now used in some capacity to step in to divert the enemy from possibly murdering his wife and children. When I speak of the enemy, I am referring to the family member who has become "off base" or demon possessed or mentally ill, and we are afraid to leave because we have been threatened to stay one minute and then threatened to leave our home the next minute. As my night travel ended now, I witnessed myself giving a lecture on domestic violence during my dream state. Getting the attention of the group of employees I was to lecture to was difficult. I was reading an article on the people killed in domestic violent rages when a middle-aged man looked up to me and said, "That article sounds like the lady who lived in Woodcrest Hills." I, with a surprised glance, responded, "That was me."

CHAPTER 36

The Aha Moment

NOW, IT IS the second and last time that I would leave Marc. The end of the marriage was so close; if I had only known just how close it really was at that time, then I could have prepared. We had lived separate lives in this great big house for so long. Marc had been polarizing his two children and their families behind my back to prepare. He would work on our two teenagers as well. He would say loudly to them, "Your mother is so sick, she thinks I am poisoning her. Can you believe that? Don't hang around with her or you will go down with her." He tried to cut each soul tie I had with everyone. Even my own children would hibernate when Marc would come home. They did not want trouble for themselves. He would scream loudly at me so the kids could hear him. I was isolated.

My friends were really there, but they could do nothing more for me. Our two biological children, now teens, just lived their lives and stayed in their rooms. Dad was gone most of the time and in his own separate private world, in his mental, emotional, and physical affair with Geoff; less business these days and more politics. My body was always cold. It was the love of my kids and dog and the support of friends that kept me alive. I prayed the rosary before I slept if Marc had not yet put a roofie in my Diet Coke before I went to bed. I would then pass out for most of the night. If he was gone when we all went to bed, I found out much later that chloroform was used on a cotton ball and put at the end of my nose if he had not drugged me in a drink. It was then that Marc would start his abuse on my body. I would wake up with either cuts, marks, or bruises. He would twist my neck, pull my neck from one side to the other, rub a rag with gasoline on my back to produce a skin burn, pull my eyelids, put his fist into my chest to hurt me and leave a bruise, and sit on me; he was a very large man! I was tortured by night, ignored or threatened by day, made fun of and called "delusional" behind my back. Yet I was traumatized to leave my children and home without all of these strange events being put back into a completed puzzle.

I always lay very still, with my arms crossed over my heart while I still slept upstairs in my own bedroom each night in fear that Marc would come storming into my room at night and do some type of physical harm to me as I slept. He had already removed the complete door handle. I had caught him storming into my upstairs bedroom early that one morning. What I was protected in not knowing was the fact that the cruel, malicious markings he had left so often on my body were from his own hand. The bruises appearing on my breasts, chest wall, and right hand left a detectable needle mark that you could see the next morning. My girlfriend had made me aware. She had asked me to look for a needle mark in the bruises that appeared on my breasts. She witnessed them in the privacy of her own home. Marc usually worked on my left side as I lay in my bed upstairs in my own bedroom.

The same girlfriend witnessed my bruised hand as I walked into a cafe to meet her for lunch. She commented with strength and sincerity in her eyes, "Satin, he is injecting you." It was like "Do something to save yourself." I had mentioned to my own doctor that I had once again awoken from my sleep with strange bruising on my breasts and right hand. Without thinking, she blurted out, "Is he injecting you?" Then she instantly regained her composure and ignored the whole subject by talking about my health report from the lab. However, you must remember that Marc had created a delusional file on his unaware wife by accompanying her to the local mental health facility and telling the psychiatrist that I hurt myself. They had agreed that there was no other logical explanation for me or my constant bruising with strange markings appearing repeatedly on my body. The skin on my back burned for seven days with vertical scratches that started at my neck and went down to lumbars 5 and 6.

My chiropractor, who had witnessed whiplash on my neck on an x ray, stated, "Satin, what did you do to yourself? Were you in a fender bender?"

I replied, "No, Marc did this while I slept." I went on to explain that I had awoken to Marc standing over me at the end of the bed. He was pulling my head from my spine to the left side and then the right side. It had resulted in a whiplash effect. I suffered considerable pain. I told the chiropractic doctor to report his findings to the local police. He said he did not want to get involved. He then consulted with his superior, who owned the clinic. I was told that I was of sound mind and that it was my job to report this abuse to the police.

When you are in a situation as this one, you are the only one who can help yourself. Everyone seems to be afraid of the husband. At least that was the case with me. Marc was a powerful, evil man with a savvy, sweet demeanor to those he wanted to fool. People either were afraid of him, were fooled by him, or accepted him as a relative. Many knew the wrath that could befall standing up to a man of his power, and his last name carried a history behind it. I guess you would say we were like a mob family. We had too much money in a short period for what the business brought to the table.

Only days before I left the marriage, I went downstairs from my bedroom upstairs; I lay down next to the man who had tried to maim me for years with injections, physical pain, and mental anguish, the pain being psychological as well. He spoke. He said, "Your strength has made me go crazy. Now I am the mentally ill one." He asked me, "How did you get so strong, Satin?" I lay as still and quiet as a mouse waiting for the cat to do something. He then spoke out the truth. He said in his normal tone, "SATIN, IT HAS BEEN ME. I HAVE DONE ALL OF THESE THINGS TO YOU." When your assailant, who is your own husband, the husband who had promised to love, cherish, and honor you, admits to you, in his own words, from his own mouth, that he has indeed tried to drive you nuts, tortured you physically with painful bodily harm, WITH INTENTION TO KILL should your body not survive the HEAVY METAL CHEMICALS HE INJECTED INTO YOU over time, VERBALLY ADMITS with HIS own WORDS, when you are ALONE with him in the house OF TORTURE, admits to you THAT HE TRIED TO KILL YOU, BUT YOU WERE TOO STRONG AND HE SAYS THAT YOUR OWN POWER WOULD NOT ALLOW HIM THE POWER TO KILL YOU, what do you say to your ASSAILANT?

I was afraid now that he would follow me out of the master bedroom. He could come at me with a needle but with defiance and strength. I, without hesitation, instantly got up and went to make coffee. Of course, the coffeemaker was "laced" with penicillin. It was the perfect drug of choice to use to kill his wife and watch her struggle to keep her throat from closing before she could get to her epinephrine injector, which she kept in her purse. It wouldn't have even saved me. The thought that it would save me gave me another placebo for another day to survive. In fact, extremely high blood pressure will ONLY come down with time. You have to sit and wait it out and hope your airway does not suffocate you. Suffocation is one of the worst deaths.

I had been living on diphenhydramine hydrochloride 25 mg tablets to keep the symptoms of suffocation away to survive my day. This day was what I recall as THE FACT-FINDING DISCLOSURE MOMENT. I remember it as being two exhausted boxers, still in the ring, who have battled it out mentally and spiritually over a long period. I ended up with post-traumatic stress syndrome and physical scars from Marc's torture as I slept in my bed in my own house.

The first "turning point," which is AWARENESS, happened unexpectedly on this early weekday morning. I now knew that Marc, WITH INTENTION, had HURT ME PHYSICALLY, EMOTIONALLY, and SPIRITUALLY, WITH SATANIC RITUALISTIC ABUSE for years. Later, I could recall the actual INCIDENTAL ACCIDENTS he had planned for my demise as well. One of them included our son, when I came home to find our home filled with poisonous gas. This being the incident I mentioned earlier when Marc had hired a different plumbing and heating company to reroute a gas line in our house. I came home to find a plastic spongelike material had been put in a "T" form to hold two gas lines together. There is not ANY licensed furnace/heating employee who would ever do this without being hired to do it intentionally.

CHAPTER 37

The Final Days in My Home

During the final days in my home, Marc got desperate and sloppy. I woke up to find that my forefinger had been punctured and squeezed, not to mention my blood had dripped on the bedsheets and the pillowcase. I also found cherry-red blood dripped on our master bathroom floor. I was assuming that the blood was mine and not another victim's. When I confronted Marc, the stranger he had become, he quickly washed the bloody items.

After the next days' stay in the emergency room out of town, I was treated for physical and mental trauma with special counseling from a hospital social worker. I had been poisoned with penicillin of which I was allergic to. Marc had slipped it into the coffeemaker the night before its use. My blood pressure was so extremely high that I was required to stay in the ER facility until it dropped dramatically. Also, I was to agree to be admitted voluntarily to a "safe house" for my protection from my husband who had murder on his mind. The catch being that I would have to consent to becoming a "vulnerable adult." With a man of his political influence and net worth, I could not take that risk. I had to depend solely on myself to leave my house for good. I had a deadline to leave by, which was only four days away! My teenage children could not be given any forewarning that I was abandoning them and the family I had raised for so long.

Doomsday for me was to be on Tuesday. We were to board a plane to Mexico for a deadly vacation. I would have become a mere statistic at the hand of my bisexual husband who was having a sexual affair with his colleague. He had to get rid of the evidence, which was me, his wife of twenty-five years. Of course there was a large sum of money over my head as well. Both men were our city councilmen as well as local businessmen. Needless to say, they were living a secret life as a gay couple while they remained married to their wives of many years.

CHAPTER 38

Tips on Survival Until You Leave

NEVER TELL YOUR significant other what you are allergic to or afraid of. Never bare your soul, never. Never sign any document that you do not read first or agree to. If he threatens you that he will divorce you, say to yourself, NOT out loud, "Okay, when," and walk away. If he says, "I will take the kids, and you will never see them because you are nuts," say to yourself, NOT out loud, "I hear ya." If he says, "I will see to it that you will be on the street," say to yourself, NOT out loud, "Which street?" and look real stupid. If he pushes or shoves and then threatens you not to call 911, go away from the house to call. This will be the MOST scary for you. At this point, he will be extremely angry and will return from jail knowing that YOU are now a THREAT to him.

You must make a plan for yourself and the kids as soon as he is in jail. This will be your escape time. Save some extra cash. Hide it in the toe part of a shoe. You could leave the home and go to a shelter for women and children or remain in your house, depending on who owns the house. If he went to jail over a holiday, say, on a Friday, you would have time to obtain a restraining order through the court. Don't wait for a holiday. Get to the courthouse to file for a restraining order. Judges are very good at getting those signed the same day. Your husband or boyfriend would not be able to return home to threaten abuse, terrify you, badger you, or cause fear in you or your children.

You know the buttons that set him off. He may be a drug user, alcoholic, or both. Drugs are drugs. If he is using prescription drugs such as Vicodin, Hydrocodone, pain medications, muscle relaxers, or amphetamines, meth, heroin, or cocaine, all of them will cause adverse reactions in him and make life a living hell for you, as you already know. They have hiding places in your house for the drugs. They crush Vicodin and Hydrocodone tablets and snort them with a straw through their nose. You will be out of the house when the mouse will play or hide the stash. They will run water up their nose to rinse it. Their eyes will be bloodshot and swollen. Their face will swell. They will become argumentative and demeaning to you when they need more to keep the high. They may have a scab or two from scratching on their face or in their hair. They will not want to eat. Use your computer to look up drug addicts and drug relapses. Read the warning signs.

You will turn him into the police for possession of narcotics in the house if you can find meth, heroin, or cocaine. Say will, NOT can. You have to keep empowering your own mind. Remember the three Bs: Be strong. Be smart. Be secretive. Repeat them to yourself over and over.

If the police do nothing on your behalf because he is a big shot in the community, or as I would call it, a big bully, call the sheriff's department or another sheriff in another county. It is good to let a different county sheriff's department know what is going on with you should you reside in a "good ole boys" precinct. Call a lawyer, even if they are the wrong kind. They can refer you to one who can give one hour of free advice.

The Battered Women's Shelter is good, but you cannot stay for a long time. Always ask God to provide a good, sound friend, male or female, who will look over your back and who will not be afraid to file a missing person's report should you disappear. If you know of your husband's hiding-out places, let someone know in advance. Take mental note where they all are: names, roads, streets, people you know of that he does know. Pay attention to whom he talks to in the wee hours of the morning in your house. Call them back. Ask questions.

If you dream during this time, get up and write down bits and pieces of what you remember. If you see a place or something bad in your dream and wake up even more scared than when you went to bed, pay close attention to whose face you cannot identify in your dream. People who are hiding from you in a dream have a reason.

Pay close attention to your spouse's change in habits. If he still has sex with you, take note if he comes up with a new position. Look in his vehicles for anything unusual. Pay attention to his mileage. Where did he go today, yesterday, and for what reason? Does the mileage match where he said he went? Often, people who are hiding something say they are going somewhere, but they go on a completely different day or time. In their head, they are not lying. Remember, your gut feeling is always right. It is your own intuition.

You can feel a warning that something is wrong around you by knowing the signs your own body gives to you. This warning actually comes from your gut area that is located two inches up from your own belly button. This is the area of the body that signals to your brain that you are experiencing a gut feeling. The forehead area of your body gives you the mental insight to look deeper into a gut feeling. Both of these separate parts of our body do different things. One gives us a sick feeling in our stomach if something is wrong. The middle lobe, found in the middle of your forehead, gives you more insight into the matter. The gut area usually relates to people who are close to us: wives, husbands, significant others, children, parents, friends, or people at work who are close to us. This does not mean that they are good for us, however. A strong gut feeling within yourself will signal to your third eye in your mind, which is the intuitive area of your brain, that you need to look further into the situation at hand.

CHAPTER 39

My Sensitivities

A S A YOUNG child, I was sensitive to picking up negative feelings as a piano is to its keyboard. I subdued these feelings, without the knowledge of doing so, by practicing my piano for a half hour daily. As I became more skilled with the keyboard instrument, playing for my own amusement became a regular habit. My parents were intelligent enough to know that my playing piano would lift their spirits as well. The lessons paid off, and I spent most of my life at the piano. I have owned three pianos in my lifetime, all of them being newly purchased just for me to enjoy. Now, that may sound a bit spoiled, but actually God knew that it would be good therapy for me.

In today's world, at the age I am, the age in which my son recently said, "You are old," I find the same peace and solace in writing as I did in playing the piano. Someday I will purchase yet another piano simply for my pleasure. I figure I will live yet another twenty years. Josh simply sees me aging because he sees me so infrequently. I remember buying my mother a magnet with a chef's face on it. It read, "Fifty and still cooking." She did not take kindly to that and felt upset.

My mommy friends are now deceased during the time I began this book. I have only one woman elder friend left. She recently asked me, "Do you think that you and Matt would like to watch a movie with us?" It stars Doris Day and Cary Grant. She was trying to sell the movie to us. Then she commented, "Do you even know who they are?" She then told me when it started, letting me know how long we should stay for our visit. It did end up that we all talked politics until eleven.

As my support system is declining, I realize just how long I have started and stopped the writing of this book! Marc has influenced his two eldest children whom I have raised. They respond only if I contact them within Facebook. Their children do not know that I raised them from the ages of nine and seven (Liana, part of the time). Matter of fact, I recently met Liana's two girls and introduced myself to them. They did not know that I existed as the person who raised their mommy! I was never mentioned to these children. Over the years, I would pick Christmas cards with a special tree decorated in colorful glitter that I thought the girls would enjoy, as I did as a child. Then the shocked moment came when I found out that I had never been mentioned by their parents to them. So did my stepdaughter hide the cards or throw them away? Maybe she told them that I was just someone whom they did not know? Marc took my stepchildren from me and their families. Then he worked on our own son Josh. Marc negatively influenced Josh's girlfriend too. That caused a rift between Josh and his gal, so Josh was convinced that he was doing the right thing by shedding his ties with me, whom he has loved all of his life. I could feel this paradigm shift permeating my atmosphere, but Josh cut off all contact with me while he was at the same time being convinced that he was a "mama's baby" should he have normal contact with his mother. So Marc befriended Anna, Josh's girlfriend, from the beginning. She always knew that she had a position with him, even though his relationship with Josh was strained. Then not-so-sweet Anna coerced Josh into thinking that he is indeed a "mama's baby," like I had always talked of Marc being.

Those words came from my mother as well. "Son, when you find the right girl, she comes first and your mother second." What he did not hear me say, however, was that you both have a relationship with your mother. Should any mother be sensitive to coercion? Of course we are. We love our kids to death. We would throw our bodies on top of them to shield them from a bullet.

CHAPTER 40

Antipersonality Disorders

MARC'S PERSONALITY DEFINITELY reflected many aspects of an antipersonality disorder. I believe Marc's disorder was derived from environmental factors, being a child who was raised solely by his unhappily married mother along with his older brother and sister. His mother was so unhappy with her emotionally missing husband that she created her own imaginary life. When I married Marc, she told me to throw away my feelings as I would not need them anymore. She kept herself busy in her women's groups and with ladies she met through her faith. Her faith was not in God but rather in the people who could help her out emotionally along the way. She was empty emotionally and awaited the person who could fill her up at that time. This left little or nothing to give to her children. Her husband spent his time at work and slept in his favorite chair until he went to bed and was again missing. He was missing physically and emotionally is the life story I was given by my mother-in-law. Her imaginary world could only supply her, not her children. They were "deprived" of true human emotion. Neither son would talk about his childhood, but Aunt Neena bore her soul to me because we trusted each other. Marc had impulsiveness and fearlessness at the same time that led him into risk-seeking behavior. Usually sociopaths have normal temperaments, but their personality disorder is more an effect of parental neglect or delinquent peers.

His father was emotionally missing from his mother, which led her to share her new belief system to her children. That belief was to create within your own mind an imaginary feeling of emotional balance stemming from a facade. This did not leave much for Marc to live on, although Marc said that his dad made time for him on the weekends while his brother could do no wrong in the eyes of the mother. His adopted sister, Aunt Neena, found herself in competition for her own father's attention in lieu of her emotionally deprived mother.

Marc's antisocial personality disorder resulted in his acting violently to all four of our children and myself. On one occasion, he grabbed his eldest son and threw him against a bedroom wall, only to drop him back down to fall on his bed. I remember him cornering his eldest daughter against the laundry room wall and his saliva flying into her face as he screamed and threatened her into doing the dishes. She was about sixteen. The two youngest children were victims of Marc randomly grabbing their necks and shaking their heads as he cupped their heads in his big hands. What did I do? I called the county social worker, but since he was a city official in Milwaukee, he was only warned of his demise should this continue. Then he bribed our youngest daughter with a $20 bill if she would not relay this incident to me! She told me and took the $20. Another lesson learned. Teach a child how to accept a bribe.

On one occasion, Marc pulled Josh's bike seat from under him as he straddled it. With such force, the seat ripped through the material of his jeans, missing his genitals by a thread! He was always angry! Roberta, my friend and neighbor, kept the jeans for evidence of his violent behavior. Lastly, he would corner me in our master bathroom against the wall with his large arms spread apart with one on each side of my head. He would then scream and spit at the same time. I would have to pull his ears from his head for release. He hit me one time with his back hand, and my head hit the side of our fireplace mantel. The right side of my face and ear was badly bruised and turned black that lasted for a week. This news got back to his mother, and it was not digested well. His behavior was erratic, as is any sociopath, and his impulsivity was high and varied. He took calculated risks to minimize evidence and exposure to his violent acts. He would pour out his loving side to the victim after his attack by telling them how much he loved them.

He could be caring and sweet, but this was before he was hiding his bisexual affair with a married man. The eldest children remembered more of that person. I remember the last person and a very long three years of sorrow after he made a conscious decision to abandon his three remaining family members: Josh, Sharnell, and myself.

Both psychopaths and sociopaths leave clues in their schemes. Little did I know that the strange happenings in my house and the physical markings on my body were from him. He told me that these painful markings I suffered were spiritual attacks being done to me by demons. He blamed these attacks on Native American medicine men whom I would seek out to understand what was going on in my home.

He would take one of my earrings and leave the other behind on my dresser or I would awaken to find blood on my pillowcase. It had dripped from his poking my finger with a lancer, used by diabetics to test their blood sugar. I found a pile of curled-up chicken feathers, which were positioned on the floor alongside our master bed. There was a ball of blonde hair found on the liquor bar. We all had dark hair. My bathrobe had a large hole cut out of the front breast area where my right breast would be positioned. All of these plans were for the purpose of driving me insane. As I would be busy talking about these strange happenings to friends, family, and others, I was kept occupied but appeared delusional or frankly nuts. So his scheme not only kept me from looking into his homosexual affairs but also made me physically and mentally exhausted; besides, now he had me defaming myself. What did he gain? Pity of course, for living with the crazy woman. My preoccupation with his schemes gave him and his gay buddy a good laugh.

Being unable to maintain normal relationships early on in our marriage, we spent time with my parents and our children. Educated and wealthy people repelled him. His friends came later with politics and favors. The side of him that was gay was delighted with his boyfriend. He later confessed that he was the girl in their relationship. The small part of him that loved me was sad, and I could feel this sad human being every minute of the day. I would ask myself, "Who is this person who is so sad?" Little did I know that it was one of his personalities. The home was gone. The two remaining children and I lived in a house. Even the children and I were not a supportive family any longer either. It was all dysfunctional. I was alone. He would try to brainwash our teenage kids. They clammed up and remained in their rooms. I smoked cigarettes and drank coffee. I was glued to the phone for the support from a caring friend. My children did not respect me. I was not their role model. I was stuck in denial and could not help myself at this point. He was a big bully who would show up, throw his weight around, and try to convince Josh and Sharnell that their mother was nuts.

Looking back, he was a homosexual monster. The definition of such "is one who takes part in a homosexual relationship for longer than six months without having sex with a woman." He denied me sex for three years. He continued to appear pleasant with the ladies, but his interest lay strictly with this one particular man. There was not any pleasant side to this stranger, liar, and thief (one who robbed me of my position as a wife and mother and defamed me in public). I became aware of his criminal position, his adulterous affair, and, yet to come, his plan to kill me, his wife. His thoughts were of violence as he announced to me how he had the ability to cut me up and put me in a box to ship to his old business friends who were located out of the country. They were to dispose of my ravaged body parts so no traces of me would be found.

CHAPTER 41

Schizophrenia

MARC ALSO SUFFERED from schizophrenia. He admitted to hearing imaginary voices that gave him commands to do evil things. He took me aside on one of our drives out of our city. As we sat in our car along a river, he said to me, "Satin, don't tell anyone this. Do you promise?" I nodded, not knowing what this could be about. He said, "I hear an evil voice in my head that tells me to do evil things."

Little did I know that it was a voice in his head that told him not to come home for the evening. It was the same voice that told him to slip me a roofie in my evening soda. It was an evil voice that told him to inject my vein on my right hand with drugs. It was that voice that told him to physically score parts of my body with wounds that burned during the day. It again was the same voice that told him to put toxic liquids in my beverages. All of this to keep me preoccupied so I did not look into his sexual identity, which was the fact that he was a closeted gay father, not my husband, who was in a steamy love affair with another city councilman.

This illness was the main trigger that set the direction for his plan of demise for me, his wife, the wife who would not accept his secrets. When his world came crashing down, I saw a broken man. His psyche was on the verge of crashing. His two worlds of being a man and a woman did not work for him any longer. His break was evident.

He sobbed for himself. He sobbed as he thought of how he had to kill me to save his reputation. He sobbed because I would no longer be his victim. Now he would have to find another one to take my place. He was so deep into the occult and had hidden his mental illnesses so long that he was tired and could not keep up his pretenses any longer. I escaped death. He has not yet escaped death, eternal that is.

It will come, like the thief in the night. The sorry plea will not be able to be heard from where he will hang alone in the wilderness, and he will wish that someone would come by to cut him down from the tree and give him a mere drink of water. The same drink that he refused his son after a hockey game. His words were "Wait till you get home." This is an empty shell of what was to be a man but fell short of what God intended for him. He is a criminal, an adulterer, a liar, a manipulator, a thief, the disgust of God and man. Schizophrenia affects about 1 percent of the world population. In the United States, only one out of 100 people, about 2.5 million, have the disease. Symptoms appear earlier in males than in females. The disease appears between thirteen and twenty-five years of age in girls. People suffering with this disease hear imaginary voices that give commands or make comments to the individual. The disease is classified as a major mood disorder with no cure.

CHAPTER 42

Munchausen Disease

I HAVE WONDERED FOR years which mental illnesses my former spouse actually had. He was diagnosed with multiple personality disorder, which includes depression, anxiety, and obsessive-compulsive disorder. He would buy as many as ten pairs of the same size and color of tennis shoes. He feared that they would not be attainable in the future. He purchased a case of toothpaste at a time. He owned multiple vehicles, up to five at a time. However, he would never lend one to anyone who needed one. He had a fetish over cleanliness. You could eat food that fell on the car floor mat. His cars and boat had to be immaculate. He scrubbed and bathed the babies during his early morning shower. Even though I cooked daily, Marc would never eat a leftover food item. That food went to our weekly cleaning lady and the rest of the family.

My insides, meaning my emotional makeup, always felt sad. I would ask myself, "Who am I feeling that is so sad?" It was Marc. I could feel his anger. When he would scream, the children and I all shook. After doing some research and putting the symptoms together, I believe that he suffered from Munchausen disease as well.

This is a factitious disorder in which the person makes himself the victim. They may contaminate their own urine samples or have the chills for no reason and constantly whine about this minor illness or that. It may be as simple as a fever. They may keep asking, "Feel me, do I have a fever?" or they need to lie down and rest with no apparent reason. Some will cut themselves for attention and pity.

I remember the morning Marc was lying in his bed and said, "Look what you did to me." He had called me over to look at his stomach which he had injected with his insulin needle. He had bruised his whole stomach.

He needed to make me look crazy by telling every colleague he had that his wife was nuts. He once called up a casual friend of mine and told her that he was taking me on a vacation so I could feel better. When I left him, he knew exactly where I was (at my girlfriend's house), and he told our kids and acquaintances that I was having a delusional episode and that the family was worried for my welfare because no one knew where I was. He went as far as to call my former coworker to say the same thing.

He appeared at my girlfriend's house the next morning to talk to me. She told him to leave and that I had left him for good. She also threatened him, saying that if he bothered us, she would handle the situation herself. She had owned a successful business and dealt with a variety of criminals who would gladly do her a favor should she need one.

How does this tie into my story? He then became the victim, the poor man who had the so-called delusional wife. The funny thing is that when I would wake up with cuts or scratches, body markings, and bruises on my body, our local mental health clinic said that I had to be doing this to myself. Only Marc and our children lived in our home. Marc vocalized his innocence in the whole ordeal. It only took one session with Marc at my side at the mental health clinic in order for them to diagnose me. He threatened them, saying that I was hurting myself or I had a dermatology problem that manifested on my body with visual cuts, marks, and bruises.

On one occasion, I awoke with red-tinted flesh on my back conducive to a sunburn. I have a photo of my back starting on the right side of my neck going down to my waist that appeared as skin that had been rubbed with an abrasive object in a crisscross pattern down to my waist. The red-tinted wounds, which were about two inches long and a half an inch wide, appeared vertically, making their way to my waist. They burned for seven days. These markings burned to the touch and felt as though I had fallen asleep in the sun. They had such a distinct pattern. With a picture of my back in my hand, I escorted my son to a doctor for an ailment. At his appointment, I casually showed the doctor the photo of my back and asked him what he thought could have caused this situation. He referred to my back as looking similar to patients who were victims from a cruel punishment that was called "Asian coin rubbing." He explained that a victim was held down against his will. Then several people dipped a coin in a solution that burned skin. The coin was then rubbed into the victim's back in a crisscross pattern in order to cause pain. The abrasions would burn for days. The wounds would react to my warm shower water and burn.

Next, my eyelids had been tampered with. I would awaken to the skin sagging considerably around only one eye. I had small burn holes above an eyebrow conducive to acid burns on skin. I had done nothing to myself. It was all weird. I lived in terror and the question of how these things keep appearing on my body. Marc pleaded his innocence, and I was the person who was looked at. I was the victim who was diagnosed with delusional disorder, even though the marks on my body were clearly visible and apparent. I got tired of being accused of hurting myself but did agree to take a drug, but only 25 mg of Seroquel. It is diagnosed for people with delusions and/or anxiety. It helped my sleep and some anxiety. However, the clinic diagnosed my delusional episode.

Years later, the psychiatrist I took my mother to for her dementia told me that it takes about 600 mg to stop a delusion. The tiny dose I took let me sleep. The most I ever took was 50 mg. The most I could ever take was up to 75 mg. So the delusional theory did NOT hold water or validity. Years later, my mother's doctor asked me why I kept going to a clinic that misdiagnosed me. I did stop after a year or so and ended up getting an apology letter from their administrator when I proved to him that I was misdiagnosed and that my minute amount of this particular drug could never stop a delusion.

How does this tie into my story? Marc became the victim. He lived with a delusional wife who spent her spare time child rearing to entertaining her spouse and his political colleagues in the normal sense plus sought out medicine workers and psychics to get a handle on who was doing what with her body as she slept. Up until last year, a local politician mentioned Marc's name and said what a wonderful politician he had been and then added, "But I heard he was married to a real nutcase," came along with it. The gentleman who was witness to the conversation just happened to be a former FBI agent in New York and knew of my situation here. He spoke the truth, and the group of men quietly departed.

People stayed aloof to him. Some shunned him. Others liked his ideas but said they did not trust him. One man who knew him well said that he could believe that Marc would attempt to poison me. He said to me, "I saw he had that part to him that would do something that you speak of." After all, the voice in his head told him to do bad things, remember?

Had Marc gotten by with pushing me off a cliff on our vacation or poisoning me on our final destination to another country, he would seek sympathy for being the poor guy who lost his wife. Had I suffered a stroke with his injections being made of high salt concentrate to raise my blood pressure, I could have been paralyzed and put into the nursing home. He would be the nice guy whom people would ask over for dinner. He would frequently say to me, "Satin, stick with me and I will give you a really good funeral."

I know that I need to give you more facts on this disease that people rarely suffer from, and I will. Many have suffered a severe trauma as a child. He did. When I had talked to his aunt following a surgical procedure he had done, which is common to homosexuals, she informed me of a traumatic experience he had that kept him hospitalized for months as a preteen. He would not talk about it. I think he was molested. Even worse, maybe by someone he knew and trusted. He refused to talk of this incident to anyone. I heard this tidbit of information from his aunt in confidence when I confided in her that Marc was having a large cyst that was located under his scrotum removed. Also, a female counselor told me that these cysts are common in homosexual men. It was poisoning his entire body.

A commonality among the victims of this disease is that they are depressed and anxious and have identity problems. Men suffer from this disease twice as often as women because they tend to have a secret life and do not share everything. They leave you to think that they are sharing with someone other than you, the spouse. They may or may not be.

They are very secretive and will not allow you to see their medical information. It is common for them to find a doctor out of town. You wonder, why are they so secretive? My spouse told me on one occasion that he heard an evil voice in his head, who told him to do evil things. I thought at that time it was strange, but he would never seek any kind of help. His answer for any personal issue regarding feelings or behaviors was for you, not him, to seek some form of therapy. I had never in my life gone to a psychiatrist until I was in the family some fifteen years later. Funny thing, only Marc and his mother were exempt from going to a doctor for mental illness. The two of them would even try to diagnose you by putting the whole idea into your head that you needed to be on a psychotropic medication similar to what my mother-in-law had previously been taking or her eldest son was prescribed for his depression. Both Marc's brother and sister reported to me that they were bothered by spirits in their head. They blamed it on their demonic mother.

Munchausen disease is somewhat rare, and children who suffer from it often have been abused and neglected as a child by one or both parents. It can simply be caused from emotional neglect, without intention—for example, the mother who is experiencing a nervous breakdown is preoccupied and the father is gone. The child had no one to turn to for emotional support and love. Eleanor, Marc's mother, would frequently ask me if Marc was like my father-in-law. She meant "Was he gay too?" The two of us would then have each other to depend on for emotional support within the family.

Eleanor talked freely about her nervous breakdown with me and the family. She stated that she could have gotten a divorce, but she didn't for the sake of the kids. Andes said nothing in response. Eleanor always gave the Catholic nuns the credit for supporting her during this difficult time. Funny thing, she was not of the faith. Again, Marc had learned many survival traits from his parents who were diverse in their thinking and who had lived somewhat separate lives.

CHAPTER 43

Necrophilia Fantasy

M ARC SEEMED TO have had a necrophilia fantasy with my body after he had put me to sleep with a roofie in my soda. He had made a statement to me once: "You are in such a deep sleep, Satin, that I could slit your throat and you would never know the difference." On one particular occasion, I came to from my sleep, to find him cradling me with his left arm but stroking my hair with his right hand. He was also running his hand over each of my fingers with slow motion and tenderness. On another occasion, I found him pushing his forefinger into the inner right side of my chest. It was not until later that I witnessed the unusual bruises that appeared one at a time on my chest in the same place at which I had seen him pushing his forefinger into these areas prior. He had made the comment often, "Satin, I love you so much when you are sleeping. You are the woman I married, when you are sleeping." He would then grasp my closed mouth in his large hand and say, "It is this little mouth that is then silent."

Ninety percent of those who have necrophilia fantasy are males. Half of them are gay. Sixty percent have a diagnosed personality disorder, and 10 percent are psychotic. When I say "fantasy," I mean that the person they are touching is not dead but rather in a "sleep state" or unconscious. These males may be attracted to the fact that the victim cannot reject, disagree, manipulate, or abuse them. They may enjoy the feeling of being completely in control.

The necrophiliac may view their sexual actions, in relation to their victim, as being loving and affectionate. Such individuals compare their actions to circumstances similar to the scene in Shakespeare's *Romeo and Juliet*, where Juliet kisses Romeo after he kills himself with poison.

Necrophilia can be quite varied, ranging from simply having a fantasy of a corpse to kissing, fondling, or performing sexual intercourse with the body. On one occasion, I distinctly recalled waking up to find semen running out of my vagina when I had not had sex prior. I was horrified and began thinking that he must have other men come into our home at night and use me for sex. Or he would simply say that I must have been raped by a "spirit"! Keep in mind that he had already gone with me to the mental health clinic when I complained of waking up to find cuts, marks, and bruises on my body. They had diagnosed me with a "delusional disorder" even though the abrasions were clearly defined on my body for them to see. This was meant to "shut me up" and make me feel "less than a person of dignity." I lived in a world of terror and bewilderment.

The lifeless condition of a body itself is the stimulus for the perverse individual.

It is possible that the fantasy of a "corpselike state of being" satisfies an abnormal desire in that the object of desire is seen to be capable of absolute subjugation, without the possibility of resistance. Necrophilia may be more prevalent than statistics imply, given the fact that the act would be carried out in secret with a victim unable to complain and given the length of time that the paraphernalia has been recognized.

Occupations related to this diagnosis are individuals who have been associated with psychopathology. Marc had gone to the university to study animal science but dropped out of school to marry his first wife. He was going into veterinary medicine!

Cognitive therapy is used for treatment for most paraphernalia along with the use of sex-drive reducing medication and assistance with improving social and sexual relations.

Forensic Psychiatry, CA; Stephen J. Hucher, MB, BS. FRCP © Psych Consultant Psychiatrist, Div. of Forensic Psychiatry, U of Toronto.

CHAPTER 44

Facts Leading Up to Diagnosis

B ESIDES BEING DIAGNOSED with OCD or obsessive personality, my ex-husband definitely was a psychopath. It has taken me much research to understand Marc's mind and how it worked in order for him to manifest an attempted murder scheme that was directed at me, his wife. I realize now that I had not yet met the "other" personality that took over his mind. He changed completely from the man I married into a murderer in thought, word, and almost deed. From the fairy-tale-like courtship, wedding, and honeymoon days spent with family and friends to my almost dying alone at the hand of Marc, who had become my estranged spouse. I was preoccupied for years in trying to figure out the cause and how to stop the strange spiritual happenings in our home.

Now it is easy to see the full view of his plans to rid himself of the wife who had figured out that he was bisexual and having an affair with another politician in our city. When I say "get rid of," I mean murder. In the early days of our marriage, we seemed to have normal problems.

He suffered from an eating disorder since he was about ten years of age. His weight had fluctuated up and down sixty pounds since we met. He had lost one hundred pounds three times in his life. His mother always overprotected her son by blaming his food addiction on the cooking habits of his wives, mainly me.

The secret was that he was gay. He had been molested by a person of interest, one who may have been his own father or close relative. Talk of a relative and statements of his own mother pointed to his father being the initiator in the beginning of his own interest in men. At the age of fourteen, his father took him to a gay bar for lunch to meet his friends. Marc ended up in a hospital for months after he had been molested by someone significant around the same time. His mother had a nervous breakdown and threatened to leave his father. It all adds up.

This led to Marc trying to drive me crazy and telling complete lies to family and associates that the woman he had married all of a sudden was delusional and crazy! Yes, he was hiding his own mental illnesses. Marc was a psychopath.

CHAPTER 45

Psychopaths vs. Sociopaths

M Y GIRLFRIEND ROBERTA and my husband, Marc, had so many similarities that I often commented on that fact to Marc. He internally knew it too. For some reason, he understood her and the way she lived her life. They both were impulsive and risk takers. They both loved but used a person at the same time. They were detached from human emotion and seemed to get depressed, but buying something put them both on a high for a while. Both were overeaters and overweight. Marc and Roberta were very intelligent and most capable of scheming any individual. Power, money, and prestige were high on their lists. They would both say that their children and spouse were important to them, but in reality, neither of them spent quality time with them on a daily basis. Both Marc and Roberta took great pride in taking a child on a vacation once per year rather than spending quality time with them at any other given time.

When I left Marc, I went to stay with Roberta for three months. Here was a man who was torturing me as I slept by physically hurting me in sadistic ways, poisoning my coffee with penicillin capsules that caused my throat to tighten and fear to set in on a daily basis. My husband not only was in an affair with a married man but worked on making the public think that I was "delusional" just as he tried to convince his first wife that she was as well. I asked myself, "Why didn't I suspect my own husband of 'foul-play' planning?" Roberta told me that she could drive over her ex-husband's new wife and simply say that she thought it was a dog! Roberta let her dog die in the backseat of her truck when she removed plants on one ninety-degree summer day! Marc, on the other hand, fed my dog rat poison. After my two-year separation from him, he called me up, saying, "You better pick up Smore. There is something wrong with her stomach, and she needs to go to a vet." I picked her up, and she hemorrhaged internally from the rat poison he fed her "with love" and petted her at the same time! Both of them had an instinct to harm or kill an animal. Later Marc had remorse. Roberta never had remorse.

I think often about the close comparison of my former husband and my fair-weather friend. This close comparison between the two people who were important in my life has led me to research two more mental disorders. Those two disorders are psychopathy and sociopathy.

Psychopathy and sociopathy are antisocial personality disorders. While both of these disorders are the result of the interactions between genetic predisposition and environmental factors, psychopathy is used when the underlying cause leans toward the hereditary factor. Sociopathy is the term used when the antisocial behavior is a result of a belief system or upbringing. In recent years, the term "psychopath" has acquired a specific meaning and the condition is more widely understood.

Psychopaths are born with temperamental differences, such as impulsiveness, cortical underarousal, and fearlessness, that lead them to risk taking behavior and the inability to internalize social norms. On the other hand, sociopaths have relatively normal temperaments, their personality disorder being more of an effect of negative sociological factors like parental neglect, delinquent peers, poverty, and extremely low or extremely high intelligence.

Antisocial personality disorder results in extremely violent acts. Even though psychiatrists often treat sociopaths and psychopaths as the same, criminologists treat them as different because of their difference in outward behavior.

COMPARISON CHART

PSYCHOPATHS	SOCIOPATHS
Both suffer from antipersonality disorder	ASPD

Treatment: Psychopathy is used to imply an innate condition of the individual. It is derived from nature vs. nature.

PSYCHOPATHS	SOCIOPATHS
Predisposition to violence: high	varied
Impulsivity: varies, generally low	high
Behavior: controlled	erratic
(tendency to participate in schemes and take calculated risks to minimize evidence or exposure)	(tendency to leave clues and acts on impulse)
tendency for premeditated crimes with controlled risk, criminal opportunism violence	tendency for impulse or opportunistic criminal behavior and excessive risk-taking, impulse or opportunistic violence
Unable to maintain normal relationships.	Tendency to appear superficially normal.
May hurt family and friends without guilt.	Often social predators. Can emphasize with close friends or family. Will feel guilt if they hurt people close to them.

Sociopaths and psychopaths are capable of forming relationships. The neurology of psychopaths makes it hard for them to feel empathy. They value relationships that benefit them but do not feel guilty about taking advantage of close friends or family.

Both psychopaths and sociopaths can be extremely charming. Sociopaths are generally capable of empathy and guilt so their "close" relationships may appear normal.

Psychopaths can be very manipulative and pernicious in their abuse of the people around them. Unlike sociopaths, they can almost be obsessively organized and give the normal in their relationships. They often form symbiotic or parasitic relationships.

CAREERS

Psychopaths have successful careers and try to make others trust them. Thus, they understand human social emotions quite well but are unable to experience them. This allows them to be master manipulators of human emotions. Sociopaths find it hard to maintain a steady job or home.

VIOLENT TENDENCIES

Even though psychopathy is characterized by impulsiveness, psychopaths are very meticulous in planning their crimes. Their crimes go undetected for a long time. Violent crimes are rare. Most psychopaths either take advantage of those around them without doing anything illegal or engage in white-collar crime, such as fraud.

A sociopath's outbreak of violence tends to be erratic and unplanned. They leave more clues.

Both sociopaths and psychopaths commit crimes because they are motivated by greed or revenge. Psychopaths feel no remorse after committing crimes because they lack to empathize.

THEY ARE SIMILAR

Both illnesses can be treated and alleviated if properly diagnosed. Treatment would involve both medication and therapy. They are labeled a sociopath if their mental condition was a result of childhood abuse. A psychopath is labeled if the condition is mainly congenital. Symptoms surface at about fifteen years of age. Initial symptoms can be cruelty to animals and lack of conscience, remorse, or guilt for hurtful actions to others at later stages of life.

There may be an intellectual understanding of appropriate social behavior but no emotional response to the actions of others. Psychopaths may also face an inability to form genuine relationships. They may show inappropriate or out-of-proportion reaction to perceived negligence.

TREATMENT

Both are mental illnesses only to be managed with drugs and therapy.

A psychotic person suffers a break from reality with delusions and hallucinations, but psychopaths are not mentally disabled and do not lose contact with reality.

REFERENCES

"The Neuroscientist Who Discovered He Was a Psychopath," *Smithsonian Magazine*

"Hare Psychopathy Checklist," Wikipedia

Letter from a psychopath sent to Jon Ronson, author of the *The Psychopath Test*

Sociopathy vs. Psychopathy, Kelly McAleer, Ph. D.

"Psychopathy vs Sociopathy: Why the Distinction Has Become Crucial," Jacob Pemment, *Psychology Today*

Psychopathy, Wikipedia

CHAPTER 46

A Choice of a Lifetime

A SHORT TIME PRIOR to leaving Marc, he boastfully commented to me that I had made the wrong choice of choosing him over making the life decision of choosing a man of future wealth whom I had met a mere nine months before meeting him.

After I graduated from college at the age of twenty-six, I was lost. Juan and I were done for good. I needed someone but didn't want anyone. Juan was going on to graduate school in another state. You couldn't blame him for everything either. My father desperately tried to get rid of him by using dark, evil energy directed to him. I was not a good choice for Juan because he needed a gal who would work to get him through school. I could not pass the state social work exam after trying twice. Remember also that Juan had proposed marriage to me at a local restaurant where we had spent our very first visit together in the parking lot in the wee hours of the morning. He had a split personality also. I loved the side of us that was in our own monogamous relationship but said no to the Juan who was this strange man that would give me an unfamiliar look at times. He could or would never stay in that personality. I had to make a life decision that tore my heart apart for many years later. He called me every year for six more years while I was married to Marc.

One summer, Juan came to my home while I was gone. He met the babysitter and my young children. I did not know who the unidentified visitor was. Our spirits found each other at the local mall. He felt intimidated and angry when I showered him with pictures of my two children. He did not reveal the fact that he was the visitor at my home. I always had a dream in my heart that he would fulfill his mission of becoming a doctor of psychology and I would be divorced from a rich man, then we would be together. Part of my intuition had come to fruition. He became a doctor of psychology, and I became the wealthy man's ex-wife. We have not reconnected since. I called him to visit and inform him that I was divorced, but he did not return the call. I could tell that he got the call because I saw a smile on his face and felt a good spark in my heart.

I had tried to play the reality of his bisexual personality down because I was naive even though his "mother friend" at work told me that he would never change. Bill's sister had told me that Bill was gay. The guys used Bill for sex occasionally. Juan was bisexual as well, I guess. I had visited him at his rented house one day after our split, only to witness him at his door with his hair all messed up. He said to me, "Bill is here." I left like I always did, my spirit knowing but my mind not understanding. My father had to have known. I believe that my own father had gay tendencies. If he exercised them, I do not know. We have not seen each other since his visit to my house well over twenty-six years ago.

CHAPTER 47

Postdivorce

TYPICALLY AFTER A divorce, it is the parent who leaves the marriage who takes the blame for filing for the divorce and starting the legal process. This has not changed. The parent with the most money or bigger family system or who uses sympathy to sway the kids is the parent who has the advantage. I had none of those. No family but the kids I made or raised were strictly what I had. I found solace with my new dog, after Marc had fed my dog rat poison to snuff her life out only one week before I would have gotten her back in the divorce.

Even though our two youngest children had initially told me that Dad had left our family before I had become aware, now I understood. Sharnell had asked me if Dad was gay when she was in junior high school. It was Easter, and Marc was not connected to any of us. As Marc pumped gas into our Mercedes, Sharnell nudged me in the car and said, "Mom, is Dad gay? Is he gay with Geoff?" I replied that I was not sure but thought he might be. Josh had complained that Dad had left our family and that he was not there anymore. Marc left me last. He left Josh first in order to have his male lover. Josh wrote a suicide letter, but I found it and took him to the suicide prevention health unit at our local hospital. He was an outpatient for a week. I was not going to lose my healthy son over a douche-bag gay husband. That was for damn sure. Then Marc had the nerve to blame Josh for our divorce. Marc is still a sick person and will always be in my eyes, as long as I live on this earth. I mean that with my whole heart too.

Sharnell would come home from school, and Marc would be sleeping in the afternoon on a weekday after having been with Geoff. He was dead to our world, and we had a home without a man in it. He would lie and dream about Geoff and his sexual affair with him. I witnessed Marc talking in his sleep about Geoff. This man should be kidnapped, put into an empty railroad boxcar, and shipped somewhere over the Rocky Mountains with a "no return sign" tattooed to his forehead.

How did Marc handle the family system after the divorce? First he divided the four kids into two groups: his two and our two. He separated the children. He told all four of the adult children that I had a boyfriend. He told my acquaintance friends that I was delusional and was having a delusional episode and that neither he nor the family knew where I was. He added that they were all worried about me. I, of course, had moved only one block down our street. He had come there to see that I was indeed there. He lied to every person he met. He defamed my name, made up a delusional mental illness diagnosis, and spread it throughout our town.

The two eldest children who were married with children did not buy the crap. The youngest son bought the "Mom left for another man" lie. Our daughter was just plain angry. Marc was mean to our two kids because they belonged to me. My blood ran through their veins. In order for the two youngest children to stay connected to the eldest two, they had to come to his side of thinking. They also had to accept the new woman he married to keep his heterosexual front going. If he did not find a woman, it would look to the family and the public that Mom was right about Dad being a homosexual. He could not face that and had told me in our private talk that he could not. What he failed to mention to all four children and the public eye was that he had intentionally tried to poison his wife on many occasions.

He failed to mention that he had tried to drive his wife nuts by taping her phone calls, hoaxing the house alarm system, harassing her with hang-up phone calls, having her followed daily, and spreading lies about his intelligent wife who raised his four kids most of the time without any input from him.

Now he has a new wife. She is his third wife. She is lied to always. He will always live as a closeted gay man who has broken up two families. When he gets caught, he simply finds another woman to lie to and give his extensive line of credit cards to. The kids stay loyal to be together and to get his inheritance. That is what it is all about. Money, inheritance, and connection are the glue that he uses to stay afloat.

God help this poor individual who has deceived so many people. I am glad that I am me and he is his ugly self. When he looks in the mirror, he can remember admitting to me that he intentionally hurt me physically, mentally, and spiritually. Oh, God, help this poor soul that is on a path to the underworld with no return.

CHAPTER 48

The "Baby" of the Family Marries

I T HAS NOW been eight years since I left Marc. It seemed like we had never parted when we were all united at Sharnell and Matt's wedding. I anxiously waited to be reunited with my family on this special day. The family did not include Marc but my stepchildren and our kids, that is. My stepchildren cannot write me online, nor do they answer my phone calls, but at the wedding we all hugged and told one another how much we loved one another. It was a reunion I lived for. Do I have to wait until Marc is dead to see the two eldest children I have raised from the ages of seven and nine?

It was a beautiful wedding. Sharnell and Matt did a wonderful job of planning and following through with their creative skills and talents. It was held in the city, and the convention center was uniquely decorated with flowers and chair covers. The decor was old fashioned with mason jars full of fragrance on each table. Marc, his wife, and his new stepdaughter were on the west side, the Addison family in the middle, and my new love, our old friends, and I on the east side.

Jake, the eldest of our four children, greeted me outside of the building as I came up the walk. We embraced, and we said our "I love yous" before we were near his dad so Marc would not see the loving greeting. Liana greeted me with her daughters as I walked into the reception area. We hugged, and I told her just how much I loved her, and she kept repeating, "Thank you." Her dad walked by and gave her a dirty look. Her two daughters were adorable, and I knew just how good of a mother she was by the closeness she shared with both of them. Her hands were always holding one of their hands or both. Emma is now nine, and Selena is five. Selena misplaced her mother for a split second later in the evening, and I found her precious hand held tightly in mine. Liana beamed as she saw me gripping Selena's little hand in mine until she arrived. It was just like it was supposed to be. Marc was the troublemaker among all of us. When he wanted to control us, he just lied about the other or made up things that were not true. When that failed, he simply hurt us satanically with threats or psychic poisonings to control us.

My stepchildren's spouses were happy to see me and talk to me as well. All of the family problems disappeared that day because there was emotion with truth, not lies from Marc. Marc did not speak to me the whole day even as we walked Sharnell down the aisle together. What surprised me the most was that he came over to me while I was talking to a guest. He stated to the guest that he still did not know why I had divorced him. He gestured by raising his hands in the air as he talked. Then, to my surprise, he stated that he had been in counseling for seven years since our divorce and was now with a new wife whom he was not compatible with. He stated that he was getting somewhat better. They had been married three years, he stated. My sons' loyalty remains with Marc, however. I have no family connections of my own left, except for Sharnell and her family. Marc carries the family weight, the bloodline, and my natural son Josh follows Marc and the Silverstein family. If I ask about my stepchildren, Alicia, Josh's girlfriend, simply says, "Don't tell your mother anything about the family, Josh."

CHAPTER 49

Time Passes

I T IS OCTOBER 8, and not just another day but rather the day I legally ended my marriage to Marc Silverstein. It is a day of peace and reminiscence about my past, present, and future as a divorced woman who survived many attempts on my life. I am now free to make it in the world alone or fail. I choose to make it and do it gracefully and successfully.

I now can look back to our house in Shorewood, Michigan, with Milwaukee to the south and Whitefish Bay to the north. We raised our children in a small town of only thirteen thousand people or so. They had attended Atwater Elementary and Shorewood High School. It was very peaceful and tranquil there. I found myself walking daily for my self-therapy along the Milwaukee River. Smore, our family dog who was a sheltie, would run ahead of me to examine the path, as if we had never been there before. What a joy she was as a companion. If a girl cannot find a friend in her husband, she can always find a friend in her dog.

We would stroll through Hubbard Park, which was noted for having been an old Indian hunting ground. In the fall and spring especially, I loved to either walk through the wind-shifting leaves at our feet or stroll down the ever-winding paths to see the new spring buds on the trees. Either season was a win-win for us. It was in this park that I would take my notebook and journal my everyday thoughts and feelings on paper. I was told by a therapist to do just that. With a rawhide bone for Smore and a soda for me, I would find a bench seat along the river and write down how I felt that particular day. I was happy for one thing, the fact that I never had to work outside of the home while I was married to Marc. This factor allowed me to rethink how this divorce would affect our blended family now that Marc had actually said, "It is like this: Geoff is the guy and I am the girl," in private of course.

ABOUT THE AUTHOR

S ATIN WAS BORN and raised the only child until she was ten years of age. Her brother was seven years old when she left home. Her father was a strict Catholic, and her mother had been raised Lutheran but had converted on behalf of her father to Catholicism. With the age difference in children, the two siblings were both raised as "only" children. She married young and divorced in her midtwenties.

At the age of twenty-six, she attended a community college for two years and then transferred to a state college. It was there that she received her BA in social work. However, she was hired by a well-known food company to sell their products. She traveled the state for five years.

Meeting the man who was to be her soul mate took place while she was a sales representative. Married now and raising a stepson, she gave birth to their son but gave up travel to be a stay-at-home mother. Three years later, she gave birth to her second child, a girl, who joined the household at the same time her stepdaughter arrived to join the new family. Adjusting to a stepfamily was quite an adventure for everyone. She became active in stepfamily support groups and became certified as a child custody and divorce mediator in their city.

Her interest took a different path as she became a cosmetologist and worked in an assisted-living facility, the same facility where she had volunteered as a pianist. It was while she was employed there that Satin searched for answers about her marriage that had become a sham. Her loyal friends and coworkers supported her as she discovered the truth about her spouse of twenty-five years.

While she was in the process of getting a divorce, she met a widower who vowed to love her once again. The relationship ended abruptly after a year when he stated that he could not move on from the death of his wife.

After casual dating, Satin met a man who helped her through the thick and thin of divorce and readjustment. They stayed companions for four years. His bipolar disorder drove them apart. It was at this time that many physical changes were taking place. She was awarded a business to run and returned back to the family home after two long years. It was at this time her husband poisoned her dog to death. The family of twenty-five years was now split up. The two eldest children were loyal to their blood father. Their two children were loyal to Satin but found themselves angry at her for breaking up the family home. Josh was out of high school, and Sharnell had completed one year of college. Josh secured a job in the city but was looking for a relationship. The family was broken apart with only Satin to blame.

Today, Satin is a published short story writer. She owns her own massage and Reiki healing business. She is a psychic medium and life coach as well. Her current relationship came in riding on a white horse and has supported her in all of her work. They enjoy each other and time together with their special dog.

Satin brings to you this story to help you on your journey to take the big step. That big step is for you to define your own situation. She hopes and dreams that this book will encourage and help millions of women to master the threshold of fear, which consumes one when planning to leave an abusive and powerful spouse.

ABOUT SATIN

S ATIN IS A psychic medium and gives intuitive guidance out of her home by phone or in person. She offers family memorial readings. She helps grieving people find closure to their loved one's death and assists them by working through grief healing techniques. She is a spiritual life coach on personal issues, adult, vulnerable adult, and child abuse. She assists in locating missing people and pets. Also, she is called to identify and teach others who have the same gifts she possesses.

Her vast background includes a degree in social work. She is certified in Swedish massage and Reiki healing work. She owns a healing business out of her home. She incorporated cranial sacral therapy into her practice in June 2014.

MEDIUMS DIFFER IN THE WAY THEY WORK

I HAVE LEARNED OVER the years that every psychic or medium works differently. Even though the popular show *Long Island Medium* has drawn a lot of attention, it creates a tendency for people to make comparisons of how we each work. We all work differently.

It does not matter "how" we arrive at our readings but rather are they accurate?

Some people think that if I don't look at them and start telling them about their "loved one," without getting any information from them, I am, indeed, a phony. Then I get into the reading and sense, see, or hear their "passed-on" loved one. I will then relay to my client what I receive. Many are surprised to find that the "terrible" person whom they thought was for sure in "hell" or what I call "limbo," "purgatory," or "the absence of God" is not! They then question my authenticity. We cannot judge the afterlife! The difficult person may have made amends with the Creator, while the "godly" person, who was not forgiving and judgmental, is not in heaven. That person will probably need to work out a few issues in "limbo" before entering the "pearly gates."

I have spiritually seen a "receiving line" of spirits in heaven welcoming a dear friend I knew who had passed unexpectedly during surgery! The spirits were standing in a straight line taking turns shaking her hand. It reminded me of Jesus as he rode a donkey on Palm Sunday on earth. The light intensity was very bright with a "gold" shimmer to it! I could feel the ecstasy of the event.

She was now in "spirit" form, about thirty-six years of age. This would have been six years younger than she actually was on the date of her death. She wore a white robe, and I could feel her spirit there. I received the news of her death a day later! We had connected spiritually on this earth. She left behind to grieve her three family members: two teenage children and a bewildered, loving husband, many other friends, relatives, and acquaintances. The husband, in later years, committed suicide.

The "left behind" spouse, significant other, child, or grandchild may think that they can accompany their "loved one" to heaven through suicide. However, it simply does not work that way.

You do not end up together or in the same place! So don't make the mistake and try it! Life itself is a miracle, and we are all here for a divine purpose. That purpose is to learn "lessons." After we learn them and our purpose is complete, God will let us pass on to a higher spiritual state! Be at peace knowing you have a purpose, and it will be revealed to you by Him if you only ask!

CONFRONTATION IN MY DREAM

I AWOKE THIS MORNING at seven. My dream was so moving and pertinent to this book that I knew I had to include it for you. The characters in this dream were Marc and me; his current wife, Betsy; and our firstborn son, Josh.

My dream relayed to me why our son Josh has become distant from me in the past year. His two siblings had contact with me until three years ago. Then any contact stopped abruptly. I had called my stepson, Jake, asking him if he would manage my stock at his company. His answer was rather that this was something Josh could now do. Word also got back to me from Josh when Jake's wife had made the comment about me, which was this: "She was only your stepmother, and I never liked her anyway."

In my dream, I see our son Josh, whom I was so very close to all of his life, being told that his mother had a mental illness called "delusional disorder." Josh looks as though he is about ten years old here. Marc is brainwashing him into thinking that his mother has a mental disorder and that if he connects to her, he too could take on this mental disorder. Marc has also aligned his two eldest children behind himself with threats about them not getting their large inheritance from him when he passes should they associate with me in any way.

In this dream, Marc and I are in an eye-to-eye confrontation with weapons. He appears much thinner here after having had an auto accident most recently. I see myself having a gun to his neck, and there is some dialogue.

I do not pull the trigger. We are in his house. His wife is not home. I confront him about his lies and deceit to me and our children. I lay into his huge ego about how he has brainwashed and threatened each child about not being able to associate with me since our divorce. I confront him on all aspects of his infidelity, his homosexual encounters throughout our marriage, and his deceitfulness about how he abused me physically, mentally, and emotionally, needless to say, publicly as well. He has two weapons at hand. One of them is a gun at the end of a cane that he points at my heart. He does not fire. The other is a small ladies' handgun he pulls out of an open handbag in the upper right drawer of his desk in the office of his home. Neither one is fired. There was so much hatred between us that it appears as quicksand around where our feet are positioned.

He is hateful and angry at the same time because I did not stay married to him and allow him to remain engaged in his affair with Geoff. He blames me for leaving and thus breaking up the family. Of course this is "so" him. He gets up from the desk and leaves the handgun in the drawer. He shuts the drawer. He then walks out of the office as I follow behind. He is carrying the cane that contains the hidden gun. I follow behind confronting him as we go into his kitchen. He turns around in disgust and points the cane into my face. He is weak, beaten down, but nonetheless his old sneaky self! Betsy, his wife, comes home and walks into the room as well. She hears my confrontational words to him about his homosexual affairs. She has a sudden facial expression of surprise but finds immediate composure. He has told her many times that I was "nuts" and that she could not believe anything I say. To my surprise, Betsy looks at me with her beady brown eyes and says to me, "I know about this." Had he cleared this with her? Or was she a good actress finding quick composure to avoid embarrassment of her acceptance of him? The two of them walk off. She follows him out of the kitchen. I find myself leaving their house through an entry area door. I walk down a set of steps on an incline to reenter my vehicle.

I ask myself, why would a woman want to stay with a man who is a bisexual, who now has heard the truth about his abuse of his former wife? There is only one answer. That answer is money and the security that money buys.

MARC TRANSPORTS ME "SPIRITUALLY" IN MY DREAM STATE

H ERE I AM living in a fairly nice
house for a divorced lady. The house
is worth less than $250,000 compared with my previous home with Marc,
which was worth $1 million. This is my home where I love to write. I share
it with my guy Matt. He came into my life one year ago today unexpectedly
through a friend's friend lining up a blind date for us. My very special yellow
Lab tries to get my attention often by nudging my right elbow up and down
while I try to relay my story to you.

Back to the dream state of last night. Marc comes to me in my sleep
and lovingly transports me with him. Remember this is the Jekyll-and-Hyde
personality of the man who tried to kill me "really" with pills that were put in
the coffeemaker and other toxic substances that were injected into the vein
on my right hand. Without my permission, he transports me to an unfamiliar
place. I am aware that it has two floors. It is not new but has spacious rooms
in the lower level. I can feel him as I did when we were first connected in love.
Now, I am wondering how I will get back to my own bed in my own house.
Also, I hope that Matt doesn't realize that the woman sleeping next to him
is on a journey away from him in the middle of the night. I am not afraid but

curious and know that I have been spiritually kidnapped during my slumber. I now know that Marc had a "love" and "hate" relationship with me.

Well, this trip was on the "love" side of things. So now I am with him, and he has my hand. We turn a corner that has a window to the outside of the house. The banister handrail has a large square post. We proceed to the first large platform step. I grab on to the large banister post and follow the handrail down to the bottom of the stairs. I sense that his new wife either lives here with him having three or four homes or visits there but is not present. I also see grandchildren, some teenage boys and girls, maybe two younger ones, a boy and girl. This place could be Marc and his wife's residence in another place that I do not know about. Marc is showing me around the lower level.

He has obsessive-compulsive disorder, and it is clearly defined on this lower level of the house. There are many rooms on this level. There is a room with a table that contained a whole city on a platform. It was as though he designed a large city and its buildings to scale. He, in the past, had done architectural drawings. These were his hobbies. Another room had old television sets with one playing a video of our young family at my parents' home when our son was three and a half and our daughter was about six months of age. Our eldest children were in junior high. The other television, playing at the same time, had a video of our wedding playing. I had always wondered what had happened to these two important tapes that I could not find. What I was witnessing was indeed similar to seeing Elvis's recreation room at his house tour in Memphis. He had about four TV sets going at the same time so he could view the different channels simultaneously. Marc and I had taken the tour together. Another room had been dedicated to his present wife. The room contained the former apartment furniture she had when he met her! The exact furniture was in its place, as though untouched. It was laid out to scale in this room, as her apartment was as he would have entered the door. Each room represented some history of his, ours, hers, and his parents who had passed on. There were rooms filled with memorabilia. This included his first bike and his parents' records from the '40s and Boy Scout badges from his scout troop.

I could see also that he was financially gracious with his new wife's grandchildren. I could see them laughing and watching a movie on a TV set designated only for their use. This lower level was very dark. The walls looked like paneling from the '70s. The area was immense! He took me "hand in hand" through each room. This is how I remembered him to be when he was still "in his right mind." I mean when he was not torn between Geoff and me. I mean acting on his "gay" side or being consistent with how we all knew him: his "straight" side.

I was worried just how I would find "home again." Our tour was done now, and he took my hand. We proceeded back up the same stairs. He was very loving and kind. He offered me the assistance of finding me a man who was of his same worth. I was surprised at his kindness to me. I thought to myself that he may have repented to God and had asked Him for forgiveness for all of his evil deeds. Then I thought how unfair it was for someone who was as "dangerous" to others as he was to slip into the "pearly gates." During a short part of our marriage, Marc had told me that he loved me and that he wanted to go where I went! It did not last long as politics made it easy for him to meet many people who did not work for their highest good. It was on that road that he met Geoff who was not only bisexual but evil as well. I could not get him away from Geoff or the influence he had over him. It was then the destruction of our marriage and my safety was threatened. You know the rest of the story.

60960012R00107

Made in the USA
Lexington, KY
24 February 2017